Lola Cashman

Lola Cashman

Inside the Zoo
with U2

My Life with the
World's Biggest Rock Band

JOHN BLAKE

Published by John Blake Publishing Ltd,
3 Bramber Court, 2 Bramber Road,
London W14 9PB, England

First published in hardback in 2003

ISBN 1 904034 94 2

British Library Cataloguing-in-Publication Data:

A catalogue record for this book is available from the British Library.

Design by ENVY

Printed in Great Britain by CPD (Wales)

1 3 5 7 9 10 8 6 4 2

Papers used by John Blake Publishing are natural, recyclable products
made from wood grown in sustainable forests. The manufacturing processes
conform to the environmental regulations of the country of origin.

Every attempt has been made to contact the relevant copyright-holders,
but some were unobtainable. We would be grateful if the appropriate
people could contact us.

*In loving memory of my dad, Yvonne, and
all the friends I lost along the way.*

Acknowledgements

I would like to thank Emma Cashman and Adam Cashman, whose constant supplies of eggs and bread and unwilting love kept me going; Gronia and Paul Callaghan for being in my life; Jessica Dunn – a big big thank you; Jenny Parrott, Joanna Weinberg, Judith Watt and Caroline Muirhead for all their encouragement and support; Jack Starr for being such a star; Brian Ferguson for all those saturday afternoons at the races; Marcel Feigel – thank you for all your help, we got there in the end; and not forgetting my ozzie pozzie David Katon – you beautiful man, I love you and thank you for saving my tooth; the darling Renshaws for making me feel part of the family; Joanna Stewart for being my mate; John

Blake for publishing my words and Adam Parfitt for editing them; and last but not least Frank and Cathy Blinco for their love, support and heaps of laughter – God bless.

Lola Cashman

Contents

He drew a circle that shut me out –
heretic, rebel, a thing to flout.

But love and I had the wit to win;
we drew a circle that took him in

EDWIN MARKHAM

Introduction

The sun was beating down through the window on to my face and head as I gazed dreamily towards the playing fields. Within the room, *The Wind in the Willows* unfolded its tale. My daydream was shattered as I was brought back from the riverbank to reality by the threatening tones of the English teacher ordering me to pay more attention.

This is one of my earliest memories, knowing that I wanted freedom – to travel the grassy riverbanks with all the adventures they had to offer, not sit behind a desk at school or in an office. When I grew up I wouldn't get a job that would keep me caged in from nine to five. There had to be more to life.

Growing up around barren and derelict parts of East

London fuelled my imagination. From our third-floor maisonette window we could see the Thames and the boats sailing on by. There I would dream about the places I would go some day. Night after night I would lie awake, mapping my escape.

The course I was charting was towards a job that had its roots in the fashion industry.

Living in the East End and the heart of the *schmutter* district, it was easy to become beguiled by the numerous clothing manufacturers' showroom windows, which, day after day, boldly displayed the latest style of dress. The process of producing a beautifully designed fashion garment from a piece of fabric had always been a source of fascination to me, although not quite enough to coax out any type of sewing skill. One manufacturer's window that always held my attention was that of the infamous Azil Nadir.

The showroom windows of his Polly Peck empire dominated a busy stretch of the main throughway known as Commercial Road. This unforgiving road ran from the top end of Aldgate right down to the original Chinatown and the old docking district known as Limehouse. Here, artfully displayed from inside Polly Peck's huge clear glass showroom windows, were rolls of fabric alongside life-size Adel Rootstein mannequins, smartly draped and hung with the manufacturer's latest fashion items. These clothes were destined for the lithe bodies of the models and stars of the era.

I attended Tower Hamlets School for Girls. It stood next door to a chicken market known as Hessel Street. This tiny stretch of soiled market road would see daily gatherings of old immigrant housewives, who had come specifically to wander among the free-roaming chickens in search of their evening meal. On spying their supper, the shoppers would yell noisily to the butcher, pointing their finger in the direction of the bird of choice. Then the swift, sharp blade of the kosher butcher's knife quickly sealed the chicken's fate.

My school not only stood next door to this antiquated market but also directly opposite Polly Peck's showroom windows. The colourful up-to-the-minute fashions screamed out from behind their windows at my bland world, and made it seem like an anachronism.

These thriving manufacturers were the lifeline of the neighbourhood, and were well known for supplying many of the trendy West End boutiques with their fashions, as well as the local community with their weekly pay cheques.

It is easy now to see how it all began.

I had applied for a position I saw advertised for the summer in the local *Hackney Gazette*. 'Fashion showroom receptionist wanted,' it read. It proved an easy conquest. Dressed from head to toe in Yves St Laurent that had fallen off the back of a lorry, I looked the part. The job was offered to me – starting immediately.

I rather liked the job and, with the owner quite smitten with me, and very little work to do, I felt I had achieved my life's ambition – that was, until my father spoilt it for me. I had been coasting along for about fortnight. Although the wagers how long I would keep hold of the position were flying about at home, I was very happy: I was getting a salary and the owner had even asked me out.

Then everything changed.

After I arrived back at work after an extended lunch (the manicure had taken longer than expected), Mr Owner stared right into my eyes and told me that he now realised who I was. Uncertain what he meant, I stared silently back at him. I didn't have to wait long before all was revealed. He asked me if I was Boot Cashman's daughter. I maintained eye contact and took my time answering his question, knowing the answer did not sound good. Once I replied that I was, my fate was sealed. I was now unemployed – not quite sacked but unemployed – without a future or a potential boyfriend.

What had happened, apparently, was that my father, a well-known character in the East End with links to the Kray brothers, had placed a hot plate of egg and chips over Mr Owner's brother-in-law's head in the course of a dispute during a game of cards. The penny had now dropped with Mr Owner who had associated my surname with that of my infamous father. All I knew was that I had lost the best – well, only – job I had ever had. And a change of surname was definitely high on my list of priorities.

It seemed my course to travel was set. It became a

feature of my life, although not quite in the way I had hoped. I would visit far-flung places between jobs – each job having been abandoned by me because it was never quite to my liking.

Travel and language being two of my father's great loves, I was encouraged to spread my wings, and, after a rather nasty early episode in a Greek prison, I continued to roam the land, eventually coming home after experiencing the States and Europe.

It was now the late 1970s, and a four-line notice advertising the post of part-time sales assistant in a hotel outlet caught my attention. The Burberry retail division required a sales person for this small unit, situated inside a classy Mayfair hotel.

I applied and secured the position.

Burberry's was one of the more unusual and established of the retail institutions. Among many other things, it was professionally run and committed to offering a service to its customers. It was also great at bringing on its staff. If you happened to be interested in textiles, management or design, under the watchful Burberry eye, any skill you had would be nurtured and developed. In between undergoing the usual retail experience, I was sent on all types of training course by the store.

One such course was about textiles and management. It was run in the Scottish Highlands, where the textile mills and soft water were renowned for producing the finest cashmere and tweeds around. I quickly became hooked. And what was meant to be short- term employment now took a completely different turn. I had not bargained on falling in love with my job. Now consumed, I began to study the role of cloth in fashion. *Vogue* and *Harpers* became my bibles, and I began watching and questioning the store's art directors, whose job it was to oversee the general displays of the Burberry image and its products. Being interested and immersed in my work resulted in an early promotion for me within the company. This made me feel like a bit of a phoney as I was receiving payment for work I enjoyed. Surely someone would find out.

It was during these early years with Burberry's that I developed an eye for detail, studying in earnest with some of the finest interior window dressers of the time. From them I learnt the art of grouping and mixing textures and materials, as well as colour. This knowledge, together with the fact that a lot of my friends were incredibly talented in one way or another – and were busy honing their skills as photographers, dancers and models – inspired me.

Eventually we pooled our talents, spending weekend after weekend creating fashion shoots where I would supply the clothes and accessories to dress a friend who desperately wanted to model. In time she did so, eventually achieving happiness, not only through her successful career, but also by becoming Mrs David Bailey.

Another of my friends would do hair and make-up while another took the pictures. What had originally started out as fun was turning into a career working as a fashion stylist.

Now armed with my very own portfolio made up of all those weekend shoots and more, I pounded the pavements in search of an agent to represent my work. The task of an agent was to make sure your portfolio was shown to as many people in the industry as possible until eventually your number came up and you were booked on a job. Getting booked for a job was not always because some hotshot photographer liked your work. It might be that some other hotshot stylist had fallen sick and a replacement was urgently needed. And that was exactly how my career got started.

With high-paid, low-prestige bookings such as catalogues taking up much of my time, I was soon flying off to exotic locations to pin, tuck and drape some inferior-quality clothes across the bodies of sophisticated models. I learnt very quickly that the most tedious jobs often paid the most, and so the lure of the catalogue companies' high fees frequently attracted the industry's most highly professional crews. Some of the best photographers and supermodels were associated with catalogue work, and now here I was working and establishing myself among them.

Once again through another person's misfortune I was asked to assist on a commercial. I was about to cross over from the world of fashion into the world of film, as well as come into contact with the late Mr Terence Donovan, one of the best-known photographers in London, who happened to be directing the commercial. After a time, I was regularly being booked by his studio for stills work, as well as by that other very fine photographer David Bailey.

Working for Bailey had to be the biggest learning curve of my entire career. If one can work for Bailey, one can stand for almost anything – although I am eternally grateful for having had the experience. Just by being in the company of the man one invariably learned.

Bailey's motto was 'divide and conquer', and that was never truer than with his crew. It was not unusual to find that two different people had been booked to do the same job. When they both turned up for the day's shoot and the confusion began, he would just turn around and say something like, 'One of you better fuck off.'

It was always bittersweet working for the man and you were certainly kept on your toes. I loved the idea that I was working with him on some brilliant projects but at the same time I was anxious, not knowing what the day had in store.

One particular day Bailey had booked me to style a French advertising campaign he was shooting for cat food. The brief was that I was to get some very sexy lingerie and slips. He emphasised that I was to get only black and enjoyed telling me 'not to be arty farty'. He wanted nothing more than a few black items. And he went out of his way to make the point, finally insulting me by saying he had no idea why he had even bothered booking me for the job, as it was so easy even the lollipop lady at the end of the road could do it, and probably for free.

I held my counsel, and off I went, gathering an assortment of expensive black lingerie. Only something told me to cover myself and also select some colourful pieces. Once back at the studio I emptied my car of my selections leaving the coloured lingerie in the boot of the car. I knew that if Bailey spotted them he would have a fit. I then proceeded to prepare and hang the other clothes for Bailey's approval. As his beady brown eyes cast their gaze across my selection, Bailey turned to me and said, 'Is that all you got? Didn't you bother to get anything with a bit of fucking colour in it?'

I never replied; it would have been useless. Instead, I went to the car and gathered together the colourful slips and silk robes that I had earlier selected and quietly brought them back into the studio. Immediately on spotting them hanging from the clothes rail, Bailey turned and said to me, 'Now that's what I pay you for! I don't want a fucking errand girl. I want somebody who uses their brain.'

And so the adventure began.

Chapter 1

First Encounters

B y now it was the early 1980s and things were falling nicely into place. I had an agent and work, and trips were pencilled in for the months ahead. These were the halcyon days: it was an exciting job working with the cream of the industry. It was all money, parties and adventure. Things were sailing merrily on, until I received an unexpected call.

My agency informed me that U2 were looking for a fashion stylist and that, having seen my portfolio, they wanted to meet with me. They had seen a video reel, documenting my work, which at the time was quite impressive: modern-style music promos, film and television commercials, photographic shots that had me working with those at the top of their profession: David

Bailey, Terence Donovan, Stephen Frears, Bruce Weber, Brad Branson, Matthew Rolston …

These were exciting and rewarding times, and I was deeply ensconced in the fashion world. Fashion shoots, fashion parties, fashion people – more work, travel and play. The thought of leaving behind that with which I had become so confident and familiar to go out on the road touring with a rock band held little attraction. Spoilt rock stars, their wives and entourage sounded like all the ingredients for a nightmare.

But my lack of interest in meeting with the band cut no ice with my agent, who gave U2's management my home number.

The call was to come on a Friday evening from their Dublin-based office, asking if I would perhaps just rendezvous with the guys for lunch. I agreed once I found it was to be in Dublin, for despite all my fancy travels I had never seen Ireland.

As the plane touched down in Dublin, I couldn't remember ever having felt so excited, although exactly why wasn't clear to me. Recalling that time now, it all seems such a squall – a whistle-stop tour of Dublin and lunch with only Bono – but I wasn't disappointed.

Bono and I had an instant and easy rapport. Not mentioning work, we spoke about Dublin and the East End of London and their working-class roots. We talked of our families. Bono was generous with his time and very informative, telling me of his love for the theatre and old-time music halls. He went into great detail about the famous Abbey Theatre and the importance of the writing that generated from Ireland. He also possesses a wicked sense of humour that had us cracking up most of the afternoon. He apologised for the absence of the other band members, explaining that their recording commitments had changed at the last minute (I was soon to discover this happened all too often). They were recording in the States.

Months later, Bono was to recount to the other band members his memories of our first meeting. He thought I was completely barking. After spending almost the entire day together, with no mention of work made between us, he had dropped me back at Dublin airport only to see me running back after the car. The driver had spotted me in his rear-view mirror and stopped. The back window came down, and Bono stared at me, perplexed, asking what was wrong.

'I can't sew,' I replied in earnest, feeling this needed articulating in case he had visions of me knocking the band up some outfits. With that I turned and strolled off, to echoes of his laughter filling the air.

Later, I was told that people were killing themselves for that job.

Back in London, things flowed on again pretty much as usual, until a letter arrived informing me that U2 wanted to have another meeting, only this time it was to be in the

States. The letter went on to explain that, if I agreed, a weekly fee would be paid to me, along with first-class travel and hotel accommodation. Hey, I could do with some sun, I thought. Why not go and check the other guys over?

It was almost two weeks since my meeting with Bono, and I couldn't really remember what he looked like. Not that he was forgettable, not at all – in fact, just the opposite. It was then I realised that all I had really been interested in on my first trip was seeing the sights. The job held no great thrills for me, and as I wasn't overly interested, I hadn't taken too much on board. When I think back now to that time, I'm amazed at my own *chutzpah*.

Once again, ticket in hand, travel arrangements secured, and this time with the promise that I would be looked after by U2's tour manager, off I went, sails ablaze.

The journey from Heathrow to Los Angeles was uneventful, but that was about to change as I boarded the six-seat Cessna plane on to Santa Fe. This was a turbulent trip, during which we were blown and thrown around the skies. I was praying that, if God just let me land safely, I would no longer take the piss, and would be seriously committed to the job in hand.

Safely on the tarmac, my eyes were on the lookout for my greeter. He was to come in the guise of a chauffeur, who was holding a big white placard with my name on it high above the crowd. The tour manager would meet me at the hotel, I thought.

At reception, tired and a little bewildered, I was handed an envelope and shown to a room. The letter inside was from the tour manager telling me to make myself comfortable and that somebody would be in contact.

After a much-needed shower I slept. When I awoke I saw a note under my door, informing me that I would be leaving for San Francisco in the morning. Travel arrangements had been made and someone would be in contact shortly. This felt slightly strange – and incredibly rude. I wondered why the tour manager couldn't take the time to at least meet me and explain in person what was happening.

I ordered room service, watched some TV and slept some more.

The following morning I continued my journey on to San Francisco where I was met and taken to a hotel. On entering my hotel room, I had noticed lying on the carpet another note. The phantom note-pusher had struck again. The note read: 'Sorry, LA tomorrow.' This made me feel pissed off not to say extremely disorientated, and I began to wonder whether Bono had a change of heart about me working with him. I decided that, if that were the case, he would have to jolly well inform me, as I wasn't going to go quietly.

Snuggled in the fresh, crisp sheets, courtesy of the Four Seasons Hotel, I lay back dreaming of my new Romany lifestyle, envisaging myself flying all around the world as a lady of leisure. But, as time passed, I become bored, so I decided to make use of some of the hotel's facilities, booking myself some relaxing therapies as well as chatting away on the phone to friends in LA.

I spoke to a close friend at the time, Paul Gobel, who is sadly no longer with us. He was a very big make-up artist, in more ways than one (about 22 stone big). What a character he was. I said, 'I'm arriving in LA tomorrow. The Sunset Marquis. Can you please come and play with me?' Paul was unable to meet me due to work commitments with Sade, but told me we would meet up in a few days.

Paul was always in demand, flying across continents just to paint the faces of the stars, from Paloma Picasso to Jerry Hall. It did not matter where in the world the celebrities were – if their faces were going to appear before a camera, be it still or moving, Paul Gobel's skill was sought. Paul could also be quite a prima donna, and very unco-operative if the mood took him. Once, when asked by a famous photographer if he could help lift a heavy bag, he snapped back, 'The heaviest thing I lift is a lipstick.' But, due to his talent, his rude behaviour was often overlooked.

When I finally checked into the Sunset Marquis, I was shown to a poolside room very near – I found out later – to the villas where the band members were staying. But I still had had no direct contact from U2, which I found increasingly disturbing. Never mind – Ms Cashman was going to go for it. All by myself, with friends out of town for a few days, I would have to play alone.

First port of call was Rodeo Drive, as a girl has to do what a girl has to do – shop.

Once back in the Sunset Marquis I relaxed and took tea beside the pool, the central fixture where the wheeling and dealing for a lot of the LA music scene takes place. I was excited to spot both Bob Dylan and Cyndi Lauper splashing around in the water. Little did I know then that in the not-too-distant future I would be hanging out in Ireland on a grassy patch beside a riverbank, chatting and drinking with the great man himself. Also around the Marquis pool was a posse of about six women, laughing and gossiping and being quite stand-offish. Later, I was to find out that they all knew who I was.

Mayhem followed with the arrival of my friend Paul, who finally made his grand entrance. Imagine this 22-stone, 6ft 2in apparition dressed from head to toe in black, looking not unlike Demis Roussos, sweeping along yelling my name and waving his outstretched arms in my direction. All eyes were now fixed on me, as he bellowed his greetings once again, 'Lola, Lola.'

At the same time an unusually tall and beautiful black woman, who was with the unfriendly posse of women, glanced towards us, and then lifted her gangly frame from her seat, as she came striding across in the direction of Paul. He had a delighted look of recognition on his face and screamed, 'Alvenia,' as they embraced. 'Alvenia,' Paul said, 'this is my very good friend, Lola Cashman.'

So it took a friend of mine, and a hint of drama, to finally introduce me to a member of the U2 entourage.

Now the ice was broken, Alvenia invited us over to her friends and introduced me to everyone. They were all members of U2's management group. To be honest, I wouldn't have minded if she hadn't as the girls were prize bitches. I thought it then and I have no reason to change my mind now. But, as I was to discover, that's part and parcel of the world of touring, as everybody's sparring for a piece of the action. I was soon to witness power struggles that would leave *I Claudius* standing.

Looking around, I wondered which one was the phantom note-pusher.

A couple of days passed. I was now very settled into the Sunset Marquis life: breakfasting around the pool, reading, swimming and truly feeling like I was on holiday. I still found it hard to believe that I had been in the States for almost six days and still hadn't met or heard from the tour manager, or any other members of the band.

But my tan was coming along nicely, and I was hanging out with Paul, Matthew Rolston the photographer, and the then up-and-coming actress Milla Jovovich. At that moment in time, life consisted of dining, frequenting the 'right' parties and generally having fun.

Then it came: a memo, summoning me to an impromptu

gig that U2 were doing in LA. Bono wanted me to watch the show and then give in a written report.

Ignored and neglected, I was now feeling savage.

That night I watched the gig. From the front of the lighting stand, pen and paper at the ready, I immersed myself in the entire show. It was exhilarating. I was totally absorbed by their performance. Although I wasn't familiar with U2's music, that wasn't what took me over. The band's visual image on stage was dowdy and, I felt, in serious need of enhancement. Recognising and noting the areas that could be encouraged and tightened to lend an even stronger stage presence, I scribbled away. I wasn't to meet the band that night, but I finally met Dennis Sheehan, the elusive tour manager.

I awoke early the following morning, swam, ate breakfast by the pool, and then went back to my room to read my notes. I lay there and re-ran the previous night's gig around in my head.

At three o'clock I got a phone call from Dennis requesting me to an audience with the four band members in Bono's villa.

Shit, was I ready for them! The rude fuckers were going to get it, and I was going to tell it like it was.

Up I trotted through the winding paths, pushing aside the overgrown foliage and sub-tropical plants. Bono's villa was secretly tucked away, shrouded by an effusion of brightly coloured and sweet-smelling bougainvillea. The door was ajar. I knocked and entered. At last ...

I inhaled and introduced myself. They were all there: Bono, Edge, Larry and Adam.

Bono was lying down on a couch, eating grapes in his white towelling Sunset Marquis bathrobe. Edge was also wearing a bathrobe. Larry and Adam were dressed in jeans and tee shirts. They all greeted me.

Larry was extremely cautious and was clocking me the whole time, Adam was fiddling about the room but eventually he came and sat down. Larry continued to lean on the kitchen worktop, arms crossed almost belligerently, ready for our first encounter.

'Well,' Bono asked, 'what did you think of the gig?'

With no need for my notes, I began my soliloquy. 'Well, Bono, if you want to continue wearing black trousers tucked into black boots, you will need to continue eating those,' I said, pointing to the grapes that he was popping into his mouth. I continued right on, explaining how he resembled a Max Wall kind of character with his current dress style, and it certainly wasn't the most flattering of looks.

Larry said defensively and in very sombre tones that he didn't think Bono looked bad, and couldn't see what difference it made. Did it matter how they dressed?

I replied that, if punters were only interested in hearing a band's music, they could stay at home and listen to it on their stereos, CD players or cassettes. But a paying audience want to be aesthetically pleased and stimulated, as well as musically satisfied. In short, audiences wanted the complete package.

I could see I had impressed them with some valid points.

Bono seemed blown away by my observations and definitely wanted me on board his ship. I had touched his Achilles' heel. He later told his management that I was the first person in a long time who wasn't afraid of them professionally and had told it to them like it was.

I knew Bono liked me. The others? Well, that was going to take a little more time.

I handed over my report to Bono, and soon after made plans for my return to London that weekend. I met up with my friends and bid them adieu.

Bono called and invited me to eat with him before I left. (They were now making up big time in the good manners department.) This conversation was very unlike our first meeting however, being totally and obsessively work-related. Bono confided to me his plans for the band, and the path he wanted them to travel. He told me how much he wanted me to work with them, and how he would be willing to give me all the support I needed or wanted.

I was very flattered, but went on to explain to him a few of my reservations, which were:

> I was earning large sums of money doing stills shoots and advertising campaigns, and unless it was financial viable I wasn't interested. I didn't want the kudos, just the dosh. (I was being lairy.)

I hated being told what to do by people, even those who were paying me my wages, let alone the people who weren't. (Like his huge entourage and management.)

I was scared of flying.

He replied:

Money – he would get it sorted.

The only people I would be answerable to were the band, although he went on to explain that I would have to fit in with the tour agenda.

And as for flying – he would hold my hand.

Before Bono had finished speaking, I was hooked. He was so charismatic and charming. I knew I wanted the job and, more importantly, that I could deliver for them what he wanted.

So I was now working for Not Us Ltd, U2's personal company.

Wow.

Chapter 2

It's Official

It was March 1987 and I was now officially working for U2, as the band's stylist and image-maker. Bono had hired me, leaving a few of the incidental points regarding the terms of my contract to be sorted out by Principal Management, U2's management company, which was headed by Paul McGuiness, the band's manager.

U2's management was clearly unhappy about Bono's lack of communication with them regarding my new position. And it was unhappy with the terms on which I had negotiated employment. But, of course, this was just a minor detail as far as they were concerned. It certainly was nothing they felt like bringing to Bono's attention. Still, unbeknown to me, Principal Management's dissatisfaction would rumble on.

I was on a real high, elated that my skills and knowledge had been sought by the biggest rock band in the world. But my augmentation was to be swiftly felled by an introduction to Ellen Darst. Ellen was Paul McGuiness's right-hand man.

This Woody Allen lookalike was the usual hirer and firer, but as it had not been her responsibility on this occasion it had left her reeling, and if that had escaped my notice she made sure I got her next message loud and clear.

On our very first meeting, which took place backstage in one of the dressing rooms of the San Diego Sports Arena (by this time the *Joshua Tree* tour was already rolling), she informed me in no uncertain terms that I was not her choice for the stylist job. There was no way that she was going to entertain a loose cannon among her staff. This referred to me being employed by Bono and the band's company Not Us Ltd, which – I was to find out much later – was a most unusual policy. Principal Management, where she was head honcho, attended to the usual staffing matters, among many other responsibilities.

The vibes in the San Diego changing room were becoming heavy, as Ellen continued to point out that if I wanted to keep the position with the band I would have to reconsider a few things, like my salary, along with reviewing the terms of my contract. I made it clear to her that I had absolutely no intention of doing this. I explained to her that as far as I was concerned one didn't negotiate after an event, and that all fears and reservations I had previously had about working with a rock band had been discussed, sorted and finalised with Bono.

Ellen had clearly mistaken me for somebody who was desperate to work with the band and I was about to inform her how wrong she was. I had taken umbrage at her tone, and with feelings of rage welling up inside of me had yelled at her, in very graphic detail, exactly what I felt she could do with her job: 'Stick it up your arse', 'Go fuck yourself', etc.

I wanted nothing more to do with what I saw as a Mickey Mouse company.

Ellen began to falter. It was obvious that she was not used to having anybody challenge her. With her posture wilting, she began to do some serious grovelling, going on to apologise to me, whilst explaining that she had not meant to upset me but was under a good deal of pressure to keep the band happy. Until now, she went on, Bono had been without a stylist. With no aesthetic input, U2 had become anxious about their image. Their forthcoming video, 'With or Without You', needed to be shot, and with the *Joshua Tree* tour already rolling, things had become desperate, leaving Bono deeply concerned and despondent.

Continuing, Ellen explained how Bono and the band needed to find the right person to work with them, somebody that could not only do a great job but whom

Bono and the rest of the boys would feel comfortable around – and most importantly somebody they would be able to trust. At that point I interjected to remind Ellen that Bono had hired my services and, along with the other band members, had sought me to work with them. Initially, I added, I had had no intention of working for what I saw as spoilt rock stars and their chiefs. I told her that I was more than happy to continue working in my field – styling commercials and fashion shoots. I also pointed out to her that she had realised my worst fears, and all within such a short period of time.

'What would it be like working with you for a year on tour?' I had asked.

After a lot of backtracking and candyfloss smiles, discussions between Bono, Paul McGuiness, Ellen and myself took place, with Bono reiterating in front of both of them that he expected me to be offered all the support I wanted or needed by their management company. My terms were eventually met without compromise and this was to be my very first mistake. It was also the first and last time that I would ever see Ellen Darst so vulnerable.

U2 were playing a few nights at the San Diego Sports Arena in California. I was grateful that the band were not legging it directly after coming off the stage, but were hanging out to play a second gig the following night, which allowed me to familiarise myself fully with their wardrobe cases for the first time. This was to include Bono and the rest of the band's personal clothes as well as their stage outfits.

The alternative would have been the roadies' set routine of deftly dismantling and then loading the tour equipment – along with the wardrobe cases filled with clothes – on to the magnificently coloured articulated tour trucks. This method of transport was used to haul the entire tour equipment across country, with its contents not to be seen again possibly for days, until they were finally unloaded at the appropriate venue, ready to restart the process over.

These procedures were legendary.

A one-night gig, at any given venue, was already starting to be dismantled by the roadies the moment the band had stepped on stage to sing their first number. The crew had a routine that waited for nothing and no one.

This was also the first time I would meet the U2 crew, and I would need to take some time to get to know their names and work positions. Although it seemed the obvious procedure as well as being courteous, it was a vital ingredient for life on the road. Knowing the right person to address with any unforeseen hiccups or favours that might be needed was critical.

Of course, I also wanted to make some friends. Life on the road can be lonely. After the Ellen Darst saga, I was eager to start endearing myself to my follow comrades. Ignorance is bliss, so they say, and how true it was, for the task that I was about to undertake was enormous. How very green I was to the world of rock'n'roll.

In the band's designated dressing room – which had been decked out to replicate all the home comforts and accommodated sofas, armchairs and a red gingham-clothed table laid out with food and drink befitting a rock star – stood six custom-built flight cases. These trunks stood alongside a large screened TV. Also in among the clutter was a pool table, videos and games that would occupy the guys during the long hours they had to spend whiling away time between the soundcheck and that night's gig.

The six flight cases standing there were over 5ft high, and the same in width and depth. They had been designed like miniature wardrobes: once unhinged, they folded out to reveal six deep drawers, and limited hanging space. Four of the flight trunks contained the band's stage and personal effects. The other two cases were mine, to be filled with essential work items from the obscure to the obvious. God knows why, but I had sewing bags that contained everything a couture seamstress would have been proud of. Only I couldn't sew.

The first thing I did upon opening U2's clothes trunks was to empty each one, wardrobe by wardrobe, placing the contents on to sheets that I had put over a space on the dressing-room floor. Eventually I replaced all the clothes in the wardrobes and appropriate drawers, neatly folded, with all the hangers and accompanying garments facing the same way. I allocated each of the drawers to accommodate knickers, socks, tee shirts and miscellaneous items.

At first I felt very self-conscious. As I opened drawer upon drawer, scanning and emptying each of its possessions, gathering together the insides of every trunk and setting the items down on to the sheets, I felt like I was prying into their personal world.

Slowly and deliberately, I scanned the contents from each of the individual wardrobes, making notes on each pile of clothes. Sifting through some of the clothes and debris that were lying there, as if trying to reveal some half-told stories, I became anxious to bin some of the more worn-out items, but thought better of it. I would wait and bring it to the attention of Bono and the other band members.

In Edge's wardrobe, the cover of a compilation of *Bob Marley's Greatest Hits* lying among an assortment of classic blues and jazz CDs caught my eye, along with about half a dozen different-coloured plectrums, some bent with wear. There was also a very nasty comb, full of yesteryear's hairs, with bits of its teeth missing. It was sitting on top of an unframed picture of two little girls smiling, who coincidentally also had some teeth missing. (I later found out they were Edge's daughters.) There were three or four beanie-type hats along with kerchiefs and empty chewing-gum wrappers that had been screwed up and hidden among the paraphernalia. These were just a few of the items sprawled out before me that were bound for the draw marked 'Miscellaneous'. The other redundant bits of crap were placed into a bin liner that I had labelled with Edge's name, waiting for him to okay its execution.

It was not too long before I had settled myself into a steady rhythm of work, helped along by the thunderous sounds of U2 singing 'With or Without You' over and over from front of stage, as they ran through the necessary soundchecks in preparation for that night's performance.

As I continued methodically cleaning the trunks of their detritus, re-assembling the clothes in an order that I felt happy with, I became slightly conscious of people to-ing and fro-ing in and out of the band's dressing room. The door of the room opened and closed, with heads peering round asking me the same question, 'Have you seen Bono?' One or two of the people occasionally introduced themselves, wishing me luck and welcoming me aboard, before they then hurried on their way.

Daydreaming while getting on with my chore, head bent over, looking inside one of the trunks, I pursued my work, mentally preparing my course of action. Changing Bono's image along with those of Edge, Larry and Adam was going to be quite an undertaking. Where would I begin? How much money would I need? When would Bono allocate me some time? As my thoughts danced around with different scenarios filling my head, I was jolted back to reality by Bono's voice asking me how I was doing.

I told Bono that there were a lot of people wanting to know his whereabouts. He laughed and said, 'Lola, there is always somebody who wants something from me.' He went on to explain that, between them, the tour manager and Principal Management left him without a free moment to think. His time was spoken for practically 24 hours a day, with his approval needed on just about everything from TV and radio interviews to photo shoots and the upcoming filming of the *Rattle and Hum* video. All this as well as constant demands from management for his autograph, so that it could be transferred on to the official photos of U2. These things were just part and parcel of the job of a 'rock star'. Bono laughed once again, adding, 'And all I thought I had to do was sing.'

Then, taking me by my hand, he led me from the dressing room towards a connecting door and into a washroom, which housed some very crude showering facilities. Here Bono explained that he needed to speak with me and that we would be well hidden and free from any interruptions from management or crew.

Seated on a wooden bench, hidden from the view of the entrance and interrupted only by the annoying sound of a dripping tap, we began to chat. Our discussion was the first of what was to become a pattern of almost daily meetings that took place between us while we toured. This particular conversation concerned an important photo shoot that was about to take place, with Bono getting very excited about the news that *Time* magazine wanted to photograph U2 for the cover of their April issue. They were to become only the third rock band ever to feature on the cover and that was some accomplishment. It also made him anxious since there were so few days in which to prepare their image and he needed to know how soon it would be before I could start shopping for U2's new clothes. Sitting opposite him, looking at his ill-fitting black jeans, which he was wearing tucked inside some horrible black boots, I was dying to say, 'Now. Immediately,' but I held back.

As he chatted away, revealing to me some of his own insecurities as well as the fact he had concerns regarding the other band members' image – or lack of it – he mentioned that he was particularly concerned by Adam's appearance, and suggested I make him my top priority. I agreed, already conscious that Adam lacked a certain presence. He seemed to me to be the odd one out in the band. Bono also intimated that I should start to forge a friendship with Larry, Adam and Edge. He was desperate for them to take some interest in U2's visual image, which to date had been neglected. Bono thought that, once they started to feel comfortable around me, they would start consulting me on their choice of clothes.

Bono was completely focused, talking and questioning me about clothes and the impact they would have on the band's image. Publicity was approaching and he wanted the new image to coincide with it. Throughout our conversation, he kept reiterating that the band's new image had a vital role to play in conquering North America. Bono and U2 were fast becoming the hottest thing in the United States of America.

Here, among the pungent smells of mould and stale damp air, I went into some detail about how I would proceed with my task, wanting to make him fully aware of how I worked, explaining that, as I knew very little about him and even less about the other band members (who at this stage I had hardly had any contact with), it was going to take a bit of time and trust on their part.

Allowing me to understand what it was about themselves that they were trying to project would help me form and develop a particular role for each of them. Establishing identities for Bono, Larry, Edge and Adam would be paramount in helping me form their new image. Even though my job was one of manipulation, I told him, friendship and trust was another thing. These would have to evolve naturally. I could not and would not force myself upon the other band members. I wanted them to want me. Agreeing, Bono devised a plan that he said would have the boys eating out of the palm of my hand.

As I sat there explaining to Bono the changes that I would begin working on, I told him that at first the differences would be hardly noticeable. But on film and footage these minor details would start to take shape and begin to enhance their look. He listened attentively as I sat and carefully explained everything to him, breaking down the effect that different-textured clothes could have and the role well-made garments played. Even if they were purchased from a vintage store, I explained, once they were re-tailored to fit, this would convey a strong image.

I went on to point out that image was not just about clothes, especially when it came to photographs. If the photo was a headshot, then I could see hats coming into play, I said, along with earrings or even a ring on the finger that could be bought to life by the pose of the subject. After I gave him several examples and Bono grasped my point, I eventually steered the conversation back round to him, putting him on the spot by quizzing him about himself. Ignoring his embarrassment and flippant replies, I continued probing him, asking questions like, 'What is it that you want to say about yourself?' 'How do you want your fans to perceive you?' 'Who are the people you admire?'

Bono cocked his head to one side as he eyed me with a puzzled expression on his face, perplexed as he now gazed down at the tiled floor, quiet for a moment as if taking time to think about what I had asked him. Looking straight back at me, he then answered by saying that he wanted to project to his fans that he was in touch with them, that he came from where they came from and was one of them.

I think not.

I assured Bono that, once I was armed with similar bits of information from the other three band members, I would proceed to shop, but in the meantime I would utilise the clothes they had, feeling confident that I could at least tighten up their dowdy image. I tried to explain to Bono that having lots of money and allowing me to race off and purchase the latest designer ensembles was certainly not what it was all about, although I did pacify him by reiterating that a shopping spree was high on my list of priorities.

We ended our meeting speaking of the band's other upcoming events, concluding that Ellen would have the U2 publicity department keep me informed of the band's publicity schedule well in advance. This would allow me time to prepare outfits and accessories that I required from each of the boys' wardrobe cases (before they had been loaded on to the trucks).

Bono was committed to our talks. But, over time, being privy to his and the other band members' candid behaviour gave me more insight into each of their personalities than any amount of dialogue could.

Chapter 3

My Saving Grace

As soon as we ended our meeting and stepped back inside the dressing room, Bono was lost to his management. They were pulling and pushing him with words of urgency from that room to somewhere yonder, leaving me with the wardrobe cases once more.

I began where I had left off, cleaning and repacking the last of the clothes trunks. It was Bono's, but you could have been forgiven for thinking it was part of WH Smith's stationery store. There were scrawled-on notepads in every nook and cranny. Even his jeans and jacket pockets were filled to overflowing with scribbled words on pieces of paper. These writing pads came in an assortment of colours and sizes. Some looked like they had seen better days: battered, with creased and worn-out covers, barely held together but for a stubborn staple.

Five identical small yellow notepads that were tightly bound with a thick rubber band seemed to have found a dark corner. I spotted them lying in the back of the trunk, squashed together on the floor in among some boots and leather jackets. I separated these small yellow books from the rest of the notepads and loose papers. For some reason they looked important to me and, assuming they were, I placed them in the top drawer of Bono's trunk, which I had designated for his knickers. I made a mental note to bring them to his attention at some stage. I was to find out later on just how important they really were.

After finally clearing the dressing-room floor of the band's possessions, each trunk now methodically arranged and waiting for some new acquisitions, I was abruptly interrupted by a broad Irish accent bidding me 'Top of the Morning.'

There, standing before me, was my saving grace – only I didn't recognise it at the time. With his hands outstretched, Mr Finton Fitzgerald made himself known to me.

'And the rest of the day to yourself,' I answered.

With that, Finton departed in the manner in which he had appeared. Quickly.

The weeks flew by and, clichéd as it sounds, I ceased to know what day of the week it was. It was irrelevant to my life on the road. My time was forever consumed by apparently unimportant concerns, such as making sure I had arranged for the band's dry cleaning and smalls to be taken care of in preparation for the next gig. If these mundane procedures were overlooked it would have major ramifications.

Keen to be efficient and organised, I had arranged earlier in the day with the Sunset Marquis Hotel's concierge (a few green bucks and a couple of U2 tickets and the world's your oyster) that, on returning from that night's gig, I would hand him the bags of laundry along with all the clothes that needed to be dry-cleaned. As I did so, he assured me they would be ready the following day around noon, which I was delighted to hear since, relieved of this task, I was free to shop. Or so I thought.

Only I had overlooked one small point. We, the U2 entourage, would be departing from the hotel at 9.30am and heading for Hollywood Burbank airfield, where our Viscount plane would be awaiting Bono, the other band members, me and a few management staff. Our next designated port of call was San Francisco. I had failed to consult my tour schedule book, which was the gospel. It is one of the most important tools for surviving life on the road. As I was to learn the hard way – and all in my very first week. The clothes were left behind and eventually forwarded on.

My normal day was as erratic as it could possibly be. When most people were safely tucked up in bed, content and satisfied from their day's labour, I was creeping around in the early hours still working, trying to wind up my chores from the previous night's gig. I would let myself into the band members' hotel suites, creep around as quietly as possible (unsure whether they were inside the room), and search about, usually in the dark, for any discarded stage clothes that I needed to have laundered. The dry-cleaning and washing became the bane of my life.

For a while.

This sneaking about at night or early mornings in the band's hotel suites thankfully only took place if we had done a runner directly from stage and venue. Then I was supposed to help Bono and the guys change out of the damp clothes and supply them with freshly laundered outfits, either in the back of the limos which were speeding us off to some private airstrip, or laid out ready for them to change into on board U2's privately hired Viscount plane.

Bono loved the idea that he was naked in the car trying to get changed into something more becoming, whilst his adoring fans sped alongside the limo desperately trying to glimpse him. He would lie there in his underpants staring out of the window, lost in his own world.

But, nine times out of ten, what actually happened was that the guys would be so hyped from their gig that smelly wet stage clothes were just par for the course, and they would wait to shower and change back at their five-star hotel where they would take full advantage of steam rooms, jacuzzis, showers and baths complete with fluffy white bath sheets. These were just a few of the luxury facilities at their disposal and they certainly beat the antiquated showering systems backstage at the venues.

All shaved and shampooed, Bono, Larry, Edge and Adam were ready to celebrate along with the rest of the U2 entourage. Every night would see a fabulous party attended by stars and celebrities, along with the wining and dining that went beforehand.

Only, in the meantime, I would still be chasing around between the band members' limos, regathering up the outfits that I had earlier placed in them or racing backwards and forwards between the boys' hotel rooms, finishing off a wardrobe mistress's chores and feeling not unlike Cinderella before she met the Prince.

I finally grasped and understood some facts about 'Life on the Road': the only routine was that there was no routine. I soon adapted, helped along by the kind assistance of Mr Finton Fitzgerald and, of course, the five-star hotel quarters where my neighbours just happened to be the biggest rock band in the world.

Finton was the band's hairdresser, who measured in at about 5ft 3in, and had a head of hair hinting at red that was religiously shaved daily, giving him a kind of ET appearance. He had suggested that, as he had very little hair to cut, he would like to assist me with some of my wardrobe tasks.

My life took on an altogether different tempo: now that I had an assistant I no longer lay awake stressed about dirty washing. And, with my energy levels preserved from no longer having to dash down hotel corridors, trying to appear as demure as ever as I raced from band member's suite to suite in pursuit of dirty washing, I said to myself, 'Rodeo Drive, here I come!' And not a day too soon...

Chapter 4

Eric Darling

'Bono's looking for you,' I was informed as I wondered around backstage.

The last thing I needed was Bono wanting to come shopping with me. He was like a little child as he pulled faces of displeasure when I tried to dissuade him, warning him that such a trip could turn into a circus. But it was to no avail and so tagging along with me down Rodeo Drive was 'yer man'.

I finally persuaded him to lose the stupid wig that did nothing to disguise him but instead made him look like a drag queen – and not a very good one at that. He was now wearing a red baseball cap that I had loaned to him, with a pair of dark glasses that were a little bit more conservative than those we are used to seeing him in.

'Lola, what about this?' Bono would cry out every few moments as he spotted something else that took his fancy. I had asked him to forget my name, telling him that he wanted me to buy anything and everything. He recognised that he was becoming a hindrance, and suggested that we took some time out from shopping and arguing over what to purchase to sit down and reassess. This we did at a nearby coffee shop.

Munching away on a bagel, Bono told me his real reasons for wanting to come shopping. Reminding me of an earlier conversation that had taken place between us, he explained how he was about to put his plan into action. Chomping away, he revealed the plot that he said would have Larry, Adam and Edge 'eating out of the palm of my hand'. He threw his head back laughing, and gleefully rubbed his hands together, knowing the impact it would have on the other boys.

The idea was that I would buy Bono clothes and toiletries solely for his own use but, instead of taking them back to the hotel, we would wait and take them with us to that day's soundcheck, which was at the LA Sports Arena.

We finished our coffees and immersed ourselves in the conspiracy, which was essentially to hit the stores and start shopping. Except that, as Bono toyed with the tab, he informed me with a little-boy-lost look that he didn't have any cash on him. I paid the bill and we left.

We entered the Versace store, as it was close by and

connected to the shopping complex that we were in. Bono and I were looking very shifty: him in jeans and an old worn-out brown leather flying jacket, with his hair tucked inside the baseball cap, and some dark glasses helping to disguise him; and me with my battered and torn-up jeans, tee shirt and dark shades. We hardly looked like affluent types.

Once inside the shop, we went our separate ways. I wanted to at least feel like I was making some astute purchases, unlike 'yer man' who seemed to want to buy anything just to be able to execute his plan.

Some very simple shirts caught my eye. As I picked them up and walked around the very pretentious store, I noticed I was being watched by what I thought was a store assistant. Turning to this person and asking for some assistance, I was asked to wait and told that somebody would be over shortly. Only nobody came. Thinking nothing more about it, I gathered together the clothes that had caught my attention and went in pursuit of Bono.

He was quietly eyeing some trousers and jackets when I approached him with my arms full of clothes. He feigned interest in my acquisitions for about two minutes, and then wandered off, leaving me alone by a chair that I had placed the clothes on. Noticing Bono was now bored, I followed him and we decided that we would move on.

As we made our descent from the stairs to the exit, Bono was stopped by a gentleman in a uniform. At first we thought he had been rumbled, and that the guy just wanted to have an autograph. But no, this man was from the store's security, and he began questioning Bono and then me. He told us that we were behaving very suspiciously.

We were finally let out of the store, vowing that as soon as we got some time we would enrol in a course to learn the art of shopping. I was annoyed with the way we had been treated and asked, before being almost evicted from the store, for the manager's business card.

Eric Darling would be hearing from me very shortly.

It's funny how another day throws a different light on things. Still dressed in torn-up jeans, cowboy boots and a plain white Calvin Klein tee shirt, the only difference was that I had combed my hair – or at least I think I had – and applied some make-up to my face. As I had rubbed my eye, some of the black mascara had smudged under it, as my driver pointed out as he pulled up alongside the complex which housed the Versace store. Pulling down my thick-rimmed, oyster-shell Rayban glasses, I stepped from the stretch limo, and entered Rodeo Drive's Versace store again.

With no greeting forthcoming from the staff, just some ridiculous posing, which seemed to be a prerequisite – as if to say, 'Look at us, we're so cool and we work here' – I walked towards the stairs and retraced my previous day's steps, wanting to retrieve some shirts and tops that I had liked. Gathering the clothes up in my arms piece by piece, allowing the hangers to dangle about me, I slowly searched the store for any other hidden treasures, followed the entire time by an immaculately dressed, effeminate looking man, who I later discovered was the store manager.

When I was satisfied that I had not only perused the shop's entire stock, but had tired out the aristocratic blond assistant who had been trailing about behind me – volunteering the price of every garment that I had touched, feeling certain that I couldn't afford them – I headed for the stairs in order to make my way to the counter.

Blondie was in hot pursuit, asking disingenuously if he could help me carry the clothes. Finally collapsing my selection of clothes on top of the black marbled counter, I declared in my finest London tones that I wanted to see the manager – Mr Eric Darling, I believed.

Blondie meekly introduced himself, looking more than a tad concerned. He asked me what the problem was. Exchanging business cards like we were about to duel, Eric read my card and nearly collapsed. I dropped his card on to the pile of clothes. Waffling on, Eric offered up the services of the entire store for Bono and the band members' convenience. But, on hearing that Bono had been in his store the previous day and had almost been accused of shoplifting, Eric steadied himself, turning a whiter shade of pale.

This was about the only time I ever pulled rank, informing Mr Darling that I would like him to deliver all the garments I had selected for approval across to the Sunset Marquis Hotel. Eric said he would deliver the clothes in person.

The band's dressing room was beginning to look like a flea market, with an array of boxes and brightly coloured bags lying all about the place. In each of the different-shaped packages were clothes that I had bought especially for Bono.

Mixed up among the Versace and other exclusive store bags that were spilling over, filled with tissue paper, were some beautiful fabrics and threads which I had now draped over the back of the chairs and sofas. I had spotted these while I was being driven along the streets of Hollywood.

A notice had caught my eye alerting the public to an American-type yard sale. I had asked my driver to stop, requesting that he pull up a little way down the street. I felt that being seen stepping out of a limousine hardly gave me much bargaining power.

I snooped about the yard hoping to procure a bargain, and was not disappointed, coming across some unused linen and silk fabric for which I paid just $10. This material was going to be stored and brought to life at a later date.

Among my more mundane but necessary buys were three dozen shiny wooden hangers (I definitely possessed the Joan Crawford attitude towards hangers). These waited patiently back at the dressing room to be swapped with the nasty bent-up wire things that were in use and were barely able to hold the boys' clothes. The wooden hangers, although stacked neatly, were lying at a dangerous angle on the floor ready to trip up some unsuspecting passer-by.

Suddenly there was an almighty thud and a bellowing voice demanding to know: 'Who put those fucking hangers there?' After which he quickly added, 'Fuck me, it looks like a fucking bordello in here. Has Bono seen this?'

I looked across at this very angry, ginger-headed man who was cursing while trying to regain his balance and composure. It's true what they say about redheads, I thought. They are fiery.

Tom Mullally was the assistant production manager and ruled backstage with an iron glove. He scared me a bit with his thin-rimmed glasses pushed right back into the ridge of his nose, giving a strict schoolmaster impression, but there was no way I was going to show my fear.

Tom laid down a few of the backstage rules. With a rhythmic beat to his Belfast accent, he began arming me with the regulations informing me:

What I could expect for the band's dressing room in relation to showering facilities and towels.

That, once the band had arrived at the venue, NOBODY was allowed into the dressing room other than the band, the band's manager and myself.

Like a sergeant-major barking out orders he laboured the point that:

Bono's, Larry's, Edge's and Adam's possessions were my responsibility. He did not want me to come crying to him if anything was lost or stolen.

The dressing room was my domain and unless I invited anyone into the area it remained restricted. It also had to be emptied of guests well in advance of the band's stage appearance.

If there were any celebrities who did not want to leave the dressing room then I would have to evict them, 'never mind who the fuck they are'.

These were his unrelenting words and, still with the rhythmic roll of the drumbeat, he continued:

Food that had been specially designated for Bono's Green Room would also be my responsibility. (But, as I was soon to find out, anybody that Bono wanted to meet was invited into the dressing room, where there were more than ample supplies of refreshment.)

Tom also pointed out to me that the production office supplied the hand towels that were needed for the band during their gigs, and made me aware that there were only certain times of the day when I should approach him for any requests.

These hand towels were an important and much-needed prop, especially for Bono who always sweated profusely on stage. The towels by the side of stage were easily accessible, allowing him to be able to mop himself up whenever he needed to.

Tom also had his own work to do and emphasised, in no uncertain terms, that he was not my fucking nanny. 'And by the way,' he continued, 'I need to allocate your meal pass, so you are able to use the backstage catering facilities.' He informed me that he would organise that as soon as he had taken my photo with a Polaroid he had to hand. 'It's for your all-area pass. Can't move about backstage without it.'

Pigs had more chance of flying than Tom did of taking my photo just at that moment. Call me vain, but I at least wanted to look like I had made an effort, and right at that moment I was looking none too hot.

As he stood before me, I made a mental note that there was no way that I was going to be on his timetable, and that small hand towels would be my very next purchase.

'Hi. My name's Lola,' I said, quizzically staring at Tom and holding out my hand, trying hard not to salute him as I waited for him to reveal to me his name, rank and serial number.

Bono was literally jumping about when he entered the dressing room, totally taken aback to see all the merchandise before him. He was like a little kid, gloating and laughing as he searched through the bags, tearing the wrappers and tissue paper free from the garments, holding them at arm's length to inspect and admire them, before dropping them back down, and repeating the process until he had emptied all the boxes and bags of their goods. More to the point, he was elated that he would now be able to put his cunning plan into action.

Bono wanted to know when I had gone shopping and, still laughing, he called me a traitor.

'Why?' I asked.

'For stepping back inside that Versace store,' he replied.

I started to laugh as well, as I began to gather up some of the tissue and wrapping paper that was littered over the dressing-room floor, manoeuvring myself around Bono who was now standing in the middle of the room unzipping his jeans in preparation for a costume fitting.

Edge wandered into the room first, startled to behold the sight of Bono twirling around dressed head-to-toe in new jeans, belt, shirt and boots. He was pouncing about, doing an imitation of a catwalk model, with his hands on either side of his hips, as he sashayed passed both Edge and Larry, who had now entered the frame.

Turning to each of them, Bono asked how they thought he looked. He continued with the jesting and really camped it up, mincing about the dressing room as he retold our Versace shopping saga complete with his impersonation of Eric Darling. By this point we were all in fits of laughter, and Larry and Edge asked in unison, 'Who the fuck was Eric?'

'The guy in Versace who nearly done me for shoplifting,' Bono replied.

The roars of laughter echoed around the room as the boys laughed and joked some more, setting spurious wagers on the validity of Eric Darling's name. Finally, all agreed that it was a typical LA out-of-work actor's pseudonym.

Edge was now trying to cajole Bono into a conversation about an earlier incident that had occurred at soundcheck, but Bono, still full of joviality, was having none of it. All he wanted to concentrate on was the new clothes. Edge, seeing both Larry and Bono so relaxed, conceded the point and joined in with the rummaging and trying on of the garments spread out before them.

Larry now commented on one of the shirts that had been tested earlier by Bono, and was encouraged by all of us to try it on for himself. Lifting the shirt that was lying askew on the stool, he held it up, inspecting it, feeling the cloth as if to ascertain its quality. Bono glanced across the room at me and winked, and then looked back at Larry, smiling, urging him to put the shirt on. Finally succumbing to its charm, Larry began to unbutton the shirt he was wearing.

The black shirt looked cool on Larry and we all agreed that he should have it. Although very simply styled, this slightly fitted shirt worked really well with Larry's Levis and black Converse boots.

Spotting a black twisted leather belt lying among the contraband, Larry bent down, lifted it up and threaded it through the hoop of his jeans. Smiling as he passed by me still struggling to fasten his new belt buckle, Larry then drifted silently from the room.

Bono's plan was being executed to perfection. He had tried on each new item of clothing, parading it about in the dressing room, bringing lots of attention to himself, especially by asking the other band members' opinions on how he looked.

At different times Edge, Larry and Adam gathered round, admiring the assortment of shirts and trousers along with the other accessories laid out before them. Having now been lured by the beautiful items, they too wanted some new clothes.

Bono had been desperate to have the other boys show interest in their outfits and be more conscious about U2's image. It had become the cause of a number of arguments between them. Without appearing overly forceful, Bono wanted his plan to work to the point where the other band members would consult me in all matters concerning their dress.

It was a clever plan. And it was working.

Edge had seated himself on the arm of the sofa, pushing to one side the draped linen fabrics and clothes. He had his arms crossed over his chest as he began to concern himself with the cost of the clothes. Questioning me, Edge asked how much money I had spent. And how much more money did I intend to spend on their outfits?

On hearing Edge's interest, Bono stopped what he was doing and walked across the room from his wardrobe trunk. He had been searching through the drawers and clothes, shouting instructions to me about certain items he felt should be binned, holding them high for all to see, while saying that he no longer liked them.

I was now wandering around the room gathering together the new clothes that had wound up all over the place, some on the tops of trunks, some lying heaped on the ground where they had been discarded, some on the backs of chairs or on the pool table.

Leaving the rest of the emptied bags and wrapping strewn across the floor, I too finally came and sat down on the couch next to Edge and Bono.

In answer to Edge's question, I began explaining that I had been allocated £10,000 for the entire tour, which was to include all their needs such as toiletries and any other miscellaneous buys. With them all in need of new clothes, it would not be enough, I said. I went on to break down the total of my allotted budget with both Bono and Edge listening attentively.

Addressing Bono, I said that with his plans for U2 to have a complete makeover, including their own personal wardrobe, I really did not see how that amount could be sufficient. I then reiterated to Edge an earlier conversation that had taken place between Bono and myself, pointing out that U2's stage, day and evening wear was all an extension of the image that they would be projecting.

But I realised that what seemed obvious to me was not to them. I had by now discovered from Edge that he, along with Larry and Adam, were of the school of thought that it didn't matter what clothes they wore – they were musicians and only concerned with their music.

By this time, Bono was on his feet and had taken to pacing the floor. Speaking animatedly and passionately, he addressed Edge – occasionally looking back to me for validation, trying to impress on him the importance of clothes. Bono urged him to take a keener interest.

Bono added that, as far as he was concerned, writing and singing great songs was just not enough, and that with my help he was going to adopt a stronger visual image for the band. He also pointed out to Edge – as if he wasn't aware of the fact – that film and video were becoming more dominant in the music market, and that U2 had to keep up if they were to keep ahead of the game. Then, adopting a more gentle tone, he asked Edge if he really wanted to look back in a few years' time and see film and video footage of U2 looking dated and old-fashioned.

Concluding his speech, Bono said if he had to take Larry, Adam and Edge forward screaming, he was going to do it. And he was unconcerned about the cost.

It had now become very clear to me that the three other band members did not see eye to eye with Bono regarding their image. But, more importantly, I also realised they had no idea that Bono had hired me to take total control of that image.

Bono had, indeed, hatched a cunning plot. He was adamant that the boys would have to alter their style of dress, and wanted them to allow me to assist them with their image, while at the same time not appearing too forceful. Bono told me, 'You catch more flies with honey.'

Chapter 5

A Bad Case of
the B52s

Not quite awake, and uncertain of the time of day or night, I answered the ringing phone by the side of my bed.

It was Finton, wanting to know why I was not down in the hotel bar as arranged. I apologised and tried hard to make him realise how exhausted I was, but it fell on deaf ears. Next thing I knew, there was a bang on my room door. It was Finton.

'Come on, missy,' Finton said, as I stood sleepy-eyed before him. 'Get into that shower and, by the time you have washed and blow-dried your hair, I will have a cold glass of champagne poured, ready and waiting for you.

'Oh Finton,' I protested, 'I'm shattered. I just want to sleep.'

Finton ignored my pitiful excuse as he pushed past me, into my room. 'Come on, party. Rock'n'roll. All work and no play makes ...'

'OK, OK,' I interrupted. 'Shit, Finton. You can talk the hind legs off a donkey – and how about blow-drying my hair for me?' I asked, teasing him now about his supposed hairdressing skills.

The endless flow of champagne, had me relaxing and talking a load of rubbish along with Finton whose own tongue was loose and wagging and was now volunteering some 'inside information'. In return for my vows of silence, he informed me that I had to watch my back. Alarmed, and perhaps somewhat paranoid, I asked him what he meant. Finton went on to explain that people within the organisation were gunning for me, and that he had heard that I was likely to be offered very little assistance. I did not understand what it all meant, and wondered how it was going to affect me.

Finton gave me a lot of advice, and warned me that I did not help myself by being such a recluse and hardly mixing with any of the crew or management. I asked him where on earth I could find the time. I went into great detail, breaking down my daily activities for him to see. I had begun to get irritated, jostling about in my seat as I continued to seek his approval – explaining that there was just no time left in my day to hang out, but also stressing that it was nothing to do with thinking myself special. I was just boring.

By the time the band came off stage, I continued, I was already exhausted and had to wind up whatever else I was doing in preparation for the following gig. 'Finton,' I protested once again, wanting him to see my reasoning and raising my voice a few octaves, 'it is around 2.30am by the time I have done for the night, as you have witnessed. I'm too knackered to party.'

But he just looked straight at me, continuing to sip at his drink, then paused for a moment to shake his head with disapproval. Clearly Finton did not agree with me as he added, 'Think about what I have told you.' He then reminded me to remember my vow, saying that I could not repeat what he told me otherwise his job was in jeopardy.

I now wanted to go to my bed. I was feeling depressed. But, just as I was about to make my excuses, Adam came along. He was buzzing, and up for a party. As he seated himself down at the table beside me, talking ten to the dozen, he insisted that both Finton and I go on to a party with him. He was having no excuses, and just to make a point, he discreetly offered Finton a wrapped gram of coke across the table, saying, 'Here. Have some of that.'

Adam then picked up my half-drunk champagne glass and drained the rest of it. Rising from the table, he started to inform us both where and when we were to meet with him, declaring that he had to rush off – he was urgently looking for Bono. Adam couldn't sit still.

It had been years since I'd been to San Francisco and, as the song goes, 'I left my heart in San Francisco.' My thoughts were of my first love, Mitch. I wondered how he was doing. Was he still out here working? I thought back to the time when, back in the late seventies, I had joined him in San Francisco to live, albeit not for very long. Mitch had been promoted through his job and as we were already living together in London there was no escape for him. He had done the gentlemanly thing and had asked me to go with him. But once in San Francisco, we created our very own earthquakes. The arguments were long and hard until eventually I fled home, heartbroken.

As I strolled down Sutter Street in the early morning mist that is so common to San Francisco, heading in the direction of my first appointment, I laughed out loud to myself now recalling a conversation I'd had a while back with Bono about all my hotel suites resembling a florist shop. I only mentioned the matter to him thinking that the hotel had mistakenly given me his suite which usually only had one colourful flower arrangement on display.

When I first entered my suite and beheld the sight of so many magnificent bouquets of flowers spilling from their vases, along with the aromatic smells filling every corner of the room, I thought there must have been some mix-up with our rooms. Then, one day, as I was sitting there quietly gathering my thoughts, a card attached to one of the bouquets caught my attention. On closer inspection I realised that every hotel room that I had been staying in had been filled with greetings and floral arrangements from the local designer shops and boutiques of that particular city.

All the cards said basically the same thing: welcome and please feel free to call on them. On the front of each card was printed the name of the store along with the manager's name and contact numbers. Then, in handwritten scribe, they went on to inform me that they would be only too pleased to make their store available for me at any time – 'P.S. Please bring Bono with you.'

When I mentioned this to Bono, he informed me that stores were very clued up about the arrivals of celebrities in their town and also familiar with the names of their entourage, which they sourced through the tour brochures that are on sale prior to their performance.

So here I was on this early morning, strolling towards the city ready to take full advantage of Comme Des Garçon's kind invitation to their San Francisco store at the time of my choosing. This I had scheduled as an early-morning appointment, and considering the ludicrous time of the day – it would be minus a few rock stars.

They say there is no such thing as a coincidence.

I had completed my successful shopping trip and was now walking back in the direction of the Four Season Hotel where we were staying. My hands were full of shopping bags containing beautiful cashmere sweaters, silk and cotton shirts and even some trendy patterned cashmere socks that I had purchased especially with Adam in mind (he had a fetish for socks).

What followed was quite extraordinary. With a sense of utter disbelief, I suddenly heard somebody calling my name from across the road. I looked over and it was Mitch, waving and yelling to me.

We were now on the same side of the street, hardly able to speak. We just stood there looking at each other for what seemed like an eternity. First, we just stared at each other from arm's length. Then we came together to hug. We were both crying. Time, it seemed, had healed our acrimonious parting.

We both kept repeating that we couldn't believe it, what an unbelievable coincidence it was. To see each other after all these years, on a nearby street, close to where we used to live together.

We went to a coffee shop and hurriedly tried to catch up before I had to get back. After we'd said goodbye, I called back to Mitch, reminding him of my instructions as to where he was to pick up the U2 tickets and backstage passes. I was dearly hoping that I would be able to catch up with him properly after the gig. As we exchanged home addresses, we promised each other that, whatever happened, we would keep in touch. But life has a funny way of taking you on its own path, and we were not destined to meet again.

I was totally engrossed in my own world as I entered the hotel lobby. Feeling high and still slightly blown away by my earlier encounter with Mitch, I was also hungry because by now it was lunchtime. Heading straight towards the elevator I started thinking about what I would order from room service.

In order to access the lift, I had to pass a complete floor-to-ceiling panelled window area that housed the hotel bar. I strode hurriedly towards an already opened elevator door. Just as I did so, I happened to glance in the direction of the clear glass panelling where my eyes suddenly made contact with Ellen Darst. She was sitting staring out from the bar. Sitting beside her were a few of U2's entourage.

I gave a slow sigh, inhaled and bearing in mind the warning that Finton had given me, stopped in my tracks and re-routed myself towards the bar, where I appeared with a mega-watt smile spread across my face, which I believe appeared through sheer terror.

'What did you say these drinks were called?' I asked Ellen as I volunteered my shot glass forward towards the bartender. Quickly downing the contents of my refilled glass once again, I agreed with Ellen and Steve that B52s were delicious.

Thinking Ellen quite nice now that we had broken bread, so to speak, I was enjoying being part of the liveliness and conversation that was taking place between the group, which included, Steve Iredale, U2's production manager, along with a few other crew and management members. In between the laughter and exchange of jokes, I suddenly began to feel very pissed. Making some feeble excuse to the group, I stood up from my stool to leave.

Ellen rose from her seat and came towards me. As she

did so, she placed her hands on my shoulders and shuffled me back down on to the empty stool, insisting that I have another shot of poison that she had now adeptly placed before me. 'Down it in one,' she laughed. 'Come on. Let's see what you limeys are made of.' As the next B52 was already lined up for me, I didn't have much of a choice. Meanwhile Ellen kept reassuring me that, although we were departing the hotel early the next day, U2 then had a few days off. 'Go with the flow,' I was told. So I did.

What I looked like when I finally stood to make my way out of the bar I can hardly bear thinking about. As I mustered all my will power for what was the usually simple task of gathering shopping bags, I was amazed to find I could stoop down to bring them together, and not topple over.

I stood back up, trying to regain my composure, holding myself tall and erect, and balancing my many bags either side of me while contemplating my journey from the bar to the lift, desperately keeping eye contact with the door of the elevator that now appeared in my line of vision.

Come on, Lola, I told myself, you can do this. I finally entered the elevator to the sounds of distant laughter flowing from the direction of the bar.

No sooner had the doors of the lift closed than I collapsed down on to my knees and began heaving, head inside one of the Comme Des Garçon bags. I began puking my insides out, retching to the motion of the lift, into and on to the very expensive clothes, moaning and groaning all the while that I wanted my mommy. (Now I knew I was drunk, that woman was the last person I wanted.) Thankfully, there was not a soul around as I crawled, still on all fours, along the hotel corridor, dragging the bags of clothes and puke along with me towards my hotel door. Fumbling about in my handbag for the key, I continued to puke intermittently.

I was amazed at the kindness shown to me the following morning by Mike Andy, one of U2's group security. One of Mike's functions was to organise the band and management's luggage to and from our destinations. This included collecting and delivering all the suitcases to and from the assigned hotels. The normal procedure the night before U2 and their entourage departed from any of the hotels was to be informed by an up-to-date travel arrangement leaflet with the time of departure from the hotel that was delivered and pushed under your hotel door by the tour travel co-ordinator. One of the things it would bring to our attention was at what time Mike would arrive at our rooms in order to warn us that we must be ready with our bags packed in preparation for luggage collection. And always underlined in indelible ink was 'Be On Time'.

Hearing no reply to his continuous knocking and banging on my room door, Mike notified the hotel reception about the situation and was eventually assisted to enter. He found me still down on my knees in the bathroom, where I had spent the entire night, head over the loo, doing that most unladylike thing: chucking up.

I was in more than an embarrassing situation. My legs had gone numb from the pins and needles that occurred through lying in one place for so long. I was terribly ill, the prognosis most likely being alcohol poisoning. Unable to move but for the kindness of Mike, which was above and beyond the call of duty, he cleaned me up, packed my bags and literally carried me to the waiting car.

I was out of action for two days.

I made a vow to myself as I lay there, convinced I had a brain tumour, that alcohol and drugs were definitely not going to be on my agenda. Anita Pallenberg I ain't.

I also made a mental note to buy Mike a thank-you gift.

Chapter 6

Larry Gets the Hump

'What the fuck is that noise?' Larry said on first entering the Rosemont Horizon dressing room.

'It's Maria Callas singing "Casta Diva",' I replied, feigning offence as I offered to switch it off now that the band had arrived to rehearse through soundcheck, acclimatising themselves back to work after a couple of days' rest. Larry insisted I left the CD playing, wanting to give Bono, Edge and Adam a laugh.

I was something of an anachronism working there amid the biggest rock'n'roll band in the world with my love of classical music, which I always had playing while I worked. I was such a lightweight and was about to give rock'n'roll a bad name unless I gave myself a pep talk and perhaps thought about re-assessing my own image.

Larry called across from where he was now lying spread out across the couch reading, asking me to fetch him some food from the backstage catering, saying that he had risen late from his bed and, having left the hotel almost immediately after waking, had no time to eat. It was now 4.30pm.

The four band members were seated in the lounge area of their dressing room, having a break from rehearsals, each one preoccupied with his own thoughts. Larry, dressed in a pair of black Levis and a white tee shirt that was stained from food spillage, was flicking through a Harley Davidson magazine as he finished off his chilli con carne, courtesy of the Chicago Stadium's catering staff. Bono was looking very Goth all dressed in black (thankfully not with his trousers tucked into boots). He was engrossed with his pen and prose and yet another notepad. Adam's dress was unmemorable, but he was in quiet conversation with Paul McGuiness about ticket sales and money, their usual talk. Edge was over at the other side of the room dressed in what I thought was a hideous patterned shirt, worn open over a white tee shirt that he had tucked into an unbelted pair of jeans. With his more redeeming features outweighing his lack of dress sense, I thought him quite adorable as he sat on the linoleum floor browsing through the bottom drawer of his wardrobe trunk that I had marked 'Miscellaneous', fingering his stacks of CDs with his heavily booted feet tapping away to some imaginary beat.

I, too, was lost in my own thoughts as I perused the updated publicity schedule recently handed to me by Ellen. After consulting the underlined dates of the schedule thoroughly, I needed to jot down some of my thoughts and remarks, and I reached across for what appeared to be one of Bono's notepads lying to hand. It was blank, so I decided to use it.

On the schedule that was handed to me were numerous requests from magazines like *Rolling Stone* and *GQ* wanting Bono and U2's picture spread across their covers. The ones that had been approved and sanctioned by Ellen's office had been underlined with an iridescent marker pen before being handed over to me, which allowed me time to prepare and put together outfits in advance of the photo shoots.

The images crafted from clothes already in each band member's wardrobe trunks would be carefully created. Having by now gained insight into the boys' characters, I felt sure that I knew what clothes they would look good in, and – more importantly – what type of look that they would be able to carry off confidently. I was determined to give U2 a really simple yet strong, raunchy image: one that projected 'We don't give a fuck.'

In pursuit of my quest, I would sometimes even tear sleeves off Bono's tee shirts or deconstruct a number of other unsuspecting items of his clothing – all to make him appear rugged and unkempt. These items, perhaps paired with an expensive mohair waistcoat or pin-striped jacket, then teamed with a pair of well-made trousers designed to look like any other generic pair of jeans, helped achieve the desired result. Add a day of stubble, top it off with a cowboy hat and the image was complete. These basic garments manipulated together were to subtly portray to the army of adoring U2 fans that they didn't give too much thought to how they looked. But they did.

With all four band members seated before me, quite an unusual event, I wanted to seize the opportunity to get their thoughts and give them mine on the upcoming photo shoots. So I interrupted the silence by walking towards them. I was desperate to have their attention before I lost one of them to walkabouts or to Joe O'Herlihy the sound engineer.

Joe was responsible for the renowned quality of sound that people always associate with U2 at every gig. The only giveaway that he had anything to do with rock'n'roll was his long black hair, which he wore pulled back into the rocker's signature ponytail. Other than that he was the regular family man, totally devoted to his wife and kids. Being a perfectionist, Joe would utilise the band's time at the soundcheck by insisting that the band run live through the night's set list, playing the same song over and over until he was fully satisfied.

On hearing my request for their attention, Larry looked up from his reading and joked that, having heard my earlier choice in music, he was afraid of what girlie type of clothes I might have sourced for him. 'Well,' I told him, 'funny you should say that,' and I beckoned him towards his wardrobe case, whereupon I pulled a pair of black chaps off a newly bought hanger.

In one of our conversations, Larry had let on to me that he was fascinated by uniforms, and was especially taken by the garb of the American motorcycle cops, who wore tight black leather trousers and jackets, finished off by the much-copied, dark-rimmed glasses. Having discovered our mutual love of motorbikes, I decided to experiment with Larry's look, wanting to give him a slight edge over the normal biker leather image. Going down a completely different avenue, I decided to buy the black leather chaps, having found them as I was browsing around the renowned gay and lesbian sex store the 'Pleasure Chest' back in Los Angeles.

At first, Larry was having none of it and would not even contemplate trying them on, accusing me of wanting to make him look like a 'fucking nancy boy'. I didn't agree, but thought it unwise to tell him where I had found them, with Larry being so macho. And, not wanting to push it, I cast them to one side, bringing to his attention some other pieces of clothing that I had selected with him in mind. It had not been difficult choosing the Harley tee shirts, nor the vintage denim Levi jacket and jeans that I had also picked up back in LA.

With the dressing room once again vacated by the boys, I continued setting things up for the night's gig, checking the set list with the confirmed playlist of songs that had now been handed to me by Joe, checking it out myself in order to be aware of any props that might be needed to accompany a particular song. Noting that the song 'Party Girl' was on the approved playlist meant that I would have to place a bottle of champagne at the side of the stage ready for the 'chosen one' to bring on during the number. After having checked out the night's celebrity guest list, Bono and the boys would select and invite one of the more attractive female celebrities onstage to bring over the champagne. The bottle would then be popped open and a toast offered by them to the audience.

Silently I jotted down notes and reminders to myself while listening to Bono, Adam and Edge, who were now back on stage with Joe rehearsing through the sound of 'With Or Without You', their number-one single. I knew Larry was not up there with them as I heard him speaking with Ellen and Dennis Sheehan, U2's tour manager, in the corridor outside the dressing room.

By this time Finton had entered the room, panting for breath as he apologised for his tardiness. He had overslept again. He started filling me in on his night's antics, while also excitedly running me through the upcoming party schedule that he had heard a few of us lucky entourage had been invited along to by Bono. Jane Fonda's home for a private party! I agreed it sounded fun and I was keen to join in, and my thoughts alarmingly began to centre around what frock I would wear.

Finton adeptly moved himself about the place,

furnishing the boys' dressing and shower rooms with toiletries, and laying out bath towels, slippers and robes.

Larry re-entered the scene, pondering having his hair cut. After a long-winded discussion with Finton and myself, he finally agreed to sit among the lotions and potions ready for his snip.

I must have been PMSing, because my thoughts started to turn mean. I was wondering to myself what is it about these fucking rock stars that they can't decide to shit or get a haircut for themselves, when my thoughts were interrupted in midstream by Larry calling my name.

As I spoke to Larry it dawned on me that damp and musty tiled shower rooms were becoming the norm for my meetings with U2. Leaning against a washbasin, having just brushed himself of all the loose fine unwanted hairs that attach themselves stubbornly to body and clothes, Larry finally agreed that he needed advice on his image, and asked me to help source him various items of clothing. He added that shirts were what he felt most comfortable wearing, and he also requested that I buy some underpants for him. Still clueless about why his or the other band members' dress had any significance, Larry was adamant that it was just another of Bono's hair-brained schemes, although he did add that he felt I was doing a good job.

I had been trying to educate Larry about the necessity and importance of visual image for ages. I passionately wanted him to understand the part it had to play for the band, and I showed him examples of the difference between a live performance and a stills photograph – boring myself as I once again repeated what seemed to me obvious but was a continual mystery to Larry. Patience had finally prevailed.

My lecture seemed to have worked when I found Larry standing before the full-length mirror admiring his reflection. Standing almost like a robot with his legs spread-eagled and his arms outstretched, he was dressed in the chaps that he had pulled over a pair of Levis and teamed with a black leather biker jacket that he wore zipped up.

Larry agreed with me that it was a striking image, although I was slightly concerned now, seeing him standing there before me looking very uncomfortable and self-conscious. I felt he was unable to pull the look off.

It could not have been more than five minutes into Larry's costume fitting when the other members of the band walked back in the dressing room, having finished the soundcheck. When they saw Larry standing there, posed like a robot, everyone commented that he looked 'like a queer' and made 'Aw Duckie' comments. Adam went a step further, reciting out loud for everyone to hear a recent story reported in the international tabloids regarding Boy George fancying Larry Mullen Jnr.

'That's it!' Larry said, finally having all his fears validated. He tore the leathers from his body and threw them across the room, almost embarrassed about having admired himself in them. He was not amused as he stormed out from the dressing room in a furious temper, just as Adam finished the Boy George story. Adam added that Boy George even had a photograph of Larry on his refrigerator door.

The dressing room reverberated with laughter as the door to the room was slammed shut.

Chapter 7

Walkabouts

The knock at my hotel door occurred at the precise moment the phone began ringing. I left my younger sister – who was filling me in with news from back home – holding, while I attended to the door.

After apologising to my sister for keeping her waiting, I assured her that I would transfer her some funds, while also reminding her of the country's time difference. I bid her farewell and attended to more imminent things that were now seated before me.

Bono was early, very early in fact, for our 9.30am meeting, which we had arranged to have over breakfast in a nearby coffee shop (the one that adjoined the corner of Bolyston Street, just across from the Four Season Hotel where we were staying).

Making his way along the hotel corridor, coming in from the previous night's shenanigans, Bono had passed my room to get to his suite and, remembering that I was an earlier riser, thought he would chance knocking, in the hope that I was awake and could speak with him.

He looked rough, sitting there stinking of whisky, dishevelled and unshaven, and I told him so. He said that he had not yet slept and began telling me about his disappearing act from the previous evening's party, along with descriptive tales about how he had managed to dodge his bodyguard.

While he'd been roaming the nearby streets, Bono told me, he had spied an unattended bicycle which he felt needed his attention, so he mounted it and cycled off around the deserted tree-lined streets of Boston. He added that he thought it quite an achievement seeing as he was minging drunk. He was relieved, he said, to be alone with himself.

This was not the first time something like this had happened. He wanted to chat, and not just about our usual topics of conversation, it seemed. Asking me about my sister, he excused himself for having overheard my earlier telephone conversation with her. What does she do? he wanted to know. Agreeing that things must be tough for a single mother, and what with being so young as well, Bono volunteered to send her some U2 tickets. I smiled to myself, knowing my sister, thinking a roll of carpet for her new council flat would be more to her liking, and steered the conversation in another direction. But he was having none of it and wanted to talk about families, and it seemed he wanted to talk about mine.

I indulged him for a little while, running him through snippets of my siblings' lives and their jobs. Bono, now grinning, said, 'Ah, that's why you never require a limo to meet you from the airport when you return home. Your brother's a bloody taxi driver.' Once again this made me smile, and I thought, If only you knew, Bono. The chances of finding my brother driving his cab around the streets of London were slim. You would be much more likely to find him in one of the many notorious late-night speillers that are dotted around town, playing a game of rummy.

'You sure I'm not keeping you from anything,' Bono repeated over and over, in maudlin tones. He was slurring his words as he asked me to order some food. Then he continued knocking back the last of the alcohol from the room's mini bar. 'Is that all right? You don't mind, do you?' he added. I assured him that I was cool. The only concern he could have possibly detected from the look on my face was about having to hand in my hotel expenses to Bob Koch, the tour accountant, who would not be too pleased about the huge bill. (It was standard procedure that one took responsibility for their personal hotel expenses, i.e. mini bar.)

Bono was very drunk by this stage, and I wanted to get him back to his own suite, but he insisted on staying until he had eaten. Now concerning himself with his weight,

Bono pushed the plate of half-eaten food away and attempted to pour some coffee. Being the more lucid of the two of us, I insisted – relieving him of the hot coffee pot – that I would play mum, and served us both.

Although it was not the most appropriate time for any serious discussions, I agreed with Bono that he had put on weight. There was no denying it, having just recently tried on some newly acquired trousers – that had been specially designed and tailored for him – he had discovered that they no longer fitted. They were a size too small.

By this time Bono was getting even more depressed and irritable, pushing his unkempt hair off his face. He was in a sorry state. Not only was he uncomfortable about his weight and height – which he had now also mentioned – but his hair was bothering him too.

I interrupted by reminding him how drunk and tired he was, gently reassuring him that's how we all feel when we go without any sleep, and advised him to go to his bed and kip. I pushed away the breakfast table – the type that doubles as a trolley used by the hotel's catering and supplied by room service – as a way of indicating that the meeting was over and he should now leave.

Bono simply moved himself across the suite into one of the other rooms containing a made-up bed on to which he proceeded to climb, resting himself against the headboard, all the while rambling on and on, filling the room with his incoherent words.

Soon Bono was sound asleep. When I went back to the room, having showered and dressed, I saw that he had crashed out fully clothed on top of the bed. He had passed out through the combination of alcohol and sheer exhaustion. I left him there snoring and, knowing there was no gig that night, went about my day.

It was good to catch up with some old school friends, who had driven down from Connecticut where they now lived. They had volunteered to take me out for the day, wanting to drive me around parts of Massachusetts. To be fortunate enough to see it in springtime with rolling verdant pastures was a treat. Peppered throughout the drive were many modern-looking structures that I was informed were new universities and their neighbouring campuses, which would eventually see thousands of students graduate from them. Massachusetts, I was told, had more universities then any other American state.

It felt good to be in a completely different environment, and to have the opportunity to spend some time with my childhood friends was great. I tried to savour our little time spent eating, drinking and laughing, knowing I had to return back to work shortly.

My friends were unable to join me back at the hotel, having to leave early for their long drive home to Connecticut, and, exhausted from my outing, I sat myself down at the hotel bar.

I was looking forward to a glass of whisky, and the time to adjust back into my surroundings. Relaxing back into my seat with its clear views of the goings-on in the foyer, I suddenly observed Ellen Darst who, alas, had also registered me.

'Oh no,' I whispered, there was absolutely no way. I started mumbling and cursing to myself but my thoughts were interrupted mid-flow as she hurried over and presented herself before me, asking if I had seen Bono.

Relieved she did not want to break any more bread and, better yet, did not want to sit and join me for a drink, I allowed her to continue explaining, frantically, that Bono was missing.

Chapter 8

I Stand Accused

Why was this day different from any other day? I was beginning to get a little impatient as I held the line, trying to get connected to England via the long-distance operator. There had been a fault on the telephone service all morning, making my task of catching up with various designers that I had commissioned almost impossible. What with the countries' time differences, they would already have swapped the confines of their studios for the local pubs and bars.

It felt like another day wasted, leaving me totally frustrated, especially by the fact that I was unable to communicate with the designer Stephen Linnard. He worked out of London and, at my request, was hastily making some black trousers that he had earlier designed for Bono, only in a larger size, as the most recently delivered pairs were now a size too small. I had been anxious to ascertain a time and date of delivery from him.

Thankfully, I was able to get connected to the other hotel rooms, assisted by the operator, who put my call through to the travel co-ordinator, asking Theresa (who worked under Ellen) to kindly organise my day's transport, placing a request for a car. Only today I asked for a limousine. I was trying out the theory of reverse psychology. My past pleas for small-town cars that would afford me inconspicuous travel had continuously gone unheeded, with a limo regularly turning up instead. I wondered what would happen if I asked for a limo. Reverse psychology worked.

Bono had been depressed for a few days. Exhaustion from the first leg of the *Joshua Tree* tour had been put forward as the cause. That and the excessive boozing had started to take their toll: his weight ballooned and his moods swings became worse. The repercussions were felt throughout – by the band as well as their entourage. Larry and Bono were not seeing eye to eye about things in general; Adam was consumed by his own secret world of drink and drugs; and Edge had matrimonial concerns.

So I was not at all surprised by Bono's request to help him source a cosmetic surgeon. He was constantly reiterating his insecurities about his appearance. On this particular day he was complaining that his stomach was bloated and the insides of his thighs were sore due to chafing, brought on by continual sweating on a hot stage.

Bono felt that some liposuction, along with a fitness trainer, could be a short-term panacea, putting him on course for a more youthful and slimmer look. In the meantime, he had promised to try and limit his alcohol consumption which he recognised was causing the bloated effect – that and his poor diet.

I agreed to look into these matters, and suggested that in the interim we would call upon the skills of a renowned American make-up artist I knew, along with an expert hair colourist (he no longer had faith in Finton, who had accidentally turned Bono's hair orange). I assured him this would go a long way towards achieving the change he was seeking. My thinking was that, if I could get the more superficial details in place, Bono would start feeling better about himself.

The fact that U2 had already started to talk about extra tour dates back in the United States at the end of the European leg of the tour had also added to Bono's anxiety. The band was already in negotiations over filming and documenting parts of the tour. (This would eventually become the *Rattle and Hum* film.) Bono urged me to help him get into shape.

Armed with this knowledge, and recognising Bono's concern with his weight, I felt it would be only polite to speak with Ellen. After all, she was part of the management, and anything concerning the band's needs was part of her job. So I brought Bono's predicament to her attention. I hoped that, by doing so, his management would be able to throw some light on a fitness trainer, and perhaps even a nutritionist.

So, it was with some surprise and trepidation that I found myself summoned to an afternoon meeting with Ellen the following day. Paul McGuiness was also in attendance. And I stood accused. I was shocked and angered by some of the suggestions that they put before me. And I conveyed my hurt in my attempt to defend myself.

First they alleged that I was infatuated with Bono. I addressed this, telling them both that I was not infatuated but just doing my job. Second, Ellen insinuated that I was having something other than a proper relationship with Bono. I was outraged. She referred to the fact that Bono was found asleep in my room back in Boston, and was livid that when she had approached me in the bar, mentioning that Bono was missing, I had not bothered telling her that he had been in my room. I fiercely defended myself, and denied any relationship with him. I repeated loud and clear, so there were no further misunderstandings, that my relationship with Bono, albeit close, was totally professional. Finally, addressing the accusation that I had overstepped my position, I urged them to take any further queries that they had involving my work with Bono, assuring them that I only ever acted under his instructions.

But the trouble was that the whole U2 organisation was very secretive. This included all the band members. Bono,

Larry, Edge and Adam would often caution me not to let any of the other band members know what they were up to. There was no communication other than the obvious within the entire U2 company.

As the meeting neared its end, the only other thing that I did was to apologise, if only for the fact that there was a lack of communication.

Ellen clearly had a lot to get off her chest, and continued ranting on – adding that I was spending far too much time with Bono, and I should not feel that this would afford me any special treatment. 'But be warned,' she said to me, there was no way I was going to instruct her or any of her staff on how best to look after Bono. 'Lola,' she said, lowering her voice, 'do you really imagine that you could take us all on?'

The tone of her voice, and what she had said, sent shivers down my spine.

Paul McGuiness, listening in, was, he said, unimpressed with reports that were getting back to him about me. One among many was my apparent demand for a limousine to transport me about town. He had also been informed by Bob Koch, the tour accountant, of my seemingly ridiculously high hotel expenses run up back in Boston by depleting the room's mini bar of its booze. Did I know, he said, that if I entertained in my room, it was at my own expense? Who did I think I was? he added. Paul finished off by warning me that I was not to think of myself as indispensable, regardless of what Bono thought about me.

On my departure from the room, Paul hastened to add that an end-of-tour bonus that was the usual thank you to crew and management would certainly not be coming my way.

Had I walked into somebody else's nightmare? I asked myself.

Thankfully, I managed to keep my composure until safely back in my suite. Once behind the security of the closed door, I began sobbing, realising I couldn't do right for doing wrong.

'Fuck them.'

Chapter 9

Last Night Of The Gigs

Bono and Edge were pretty laid back, seated quietly, seeming to enjoy the afternoon journey from the New York hotel where we had been staying across to New Jersey on course for the afternoon soundcheck. We were all silent as we were driven along, beguiled by the spring sunshine that was indiscriminately dancing and reflecting its rays of light off of all that it touched.

Bono had asked the chauffeur to turn off the music that had been filtering through from the front of the car. Edge and Bono were staring out from the back of the limousine's window, occasionally turning to speak with one another, commenting on the beautiful weather but agreeing that they were glad that they had wrapped up warm as it was bitterly cold.

I was just sitting there quietly, studying them both, not for any particular reason, it was just that there wasn't much else to look at.

Bono was fidgeting about with his hands. He did this a lot, this thing where he interlocks his fingers. I was never quite sure if it was through habit or nerves, but right then I assumed habit, as he stared from the window, lost in thought, continually pulling and twisting away at his fingers. Occasionally, he stared down at them as if to check that they were still attached to his hands.

We all agreed it was a good idea, leaving early to get to the soundcheck, as we were stuck in horrendous traffic. The limo was barely crawling along despite the chauffeur's best efforts to avoid the jam. He even attempted a detour, which found us now on the Tri-State Bridge, still unable to move.

Bono and Edge were now involved in conversation about cars and motorbikes, with Bono revealing that he missed riding his Harley Davidson, and was going to see if he could do something about it. He knew damned well that he couldn't. It was firmly mentioned in U2's insurance policy that it was forbidden for the U2 band members to participate in any dangerous sports.

Edge, intermittently glancing out from his side of the car window, spotted an old Camero car, just yards ahead. The car was not difficult to notice: it was billowing black smoke from its exhaust. This old heap of a thing was painted primer grey and was a complete rustbucket, absolutely worthless to anyone but the driver.

With nowhere to go and the traffic at virtual standstill they had plenty of time to joke and convince each other of its marvels. Bono and Edge agreed with each other about the freedom this type of inconspicuous travel would afford them out at the Hamptons, where each of the band members had rented homes.

Approaching closer to the car, Edge noticed the 'For Sale' sign stuck to the window, which sealed its fate. Bono instructed his minder, John Singleton, who was seated alongside the chauffeur in the front, and had been listening, somewhat amused, to the pair's conversation, to jump out and broker a deal with the car's owner.

Bono had draped himself across Edge's lap, which allowed him to hang his head out of the car window. They both now had clear visibility to witness the minder's negotiating skills. Laughing and joking among themselves, they called me over to the window with them, insisting I too watch the spectacle.

On having to ascertain a price for the car, John beckoned Bono and Edge over to the smoking car and informed them that for $200 the smoking pile of shite was theirs.

The look of disbelief on the driver's face as he got out of the car was priceless. Handing over the keys to Bono he looked absolutely dumbstruck. His mouth was agape and he seemed too stunned for words as he stared first at

Bono then at Edge, repeating over and over, 'Unreal, man.'

He was not the only one in shock, as by this time some over excited fans who were also stuck in the traffic jam had noticed what was happening, and had deserted their cars to run across to Bono and Edge, wanting their autographs. Some fans were even pleading for tickets to the gig, complaining that they were unable to buy any as they had sold out so fast.

With no autographs signed for fear of a stampede, the boys legged it back into the limousine on the advice of their minder, leaving John to deal with the fans and negotiate his journey to the stadium in one very dodgy-looking car.

I was feeling happy and excited, looking forward to the fortnight's break that U2 and their entourage were taking before continuing on with the second leg of the *Joshua Tree* tour, when I was interrupted in the middle of packing by a phone call from Bono. He asked if I could join him in his suite. He needed to speak with me as soon as possible.

He was in high spirits, and when I entered the room the CD player was pumping out the sound of Van Morrison.

The band had played the last of their American gigs the previous night over in New Jersey at the Brendon Byrne Stadium, so I understood why he should be feeling so good. The gig had gone down a storm, ending with thunderous applause that filled the stadium for almost 15 minutes. The atmosphere in the arena was dynamite – it was the type that sends goosebumps down your spine and brings tears to your eyes, with nobody wanting to leave the stage. Finally, and only after an on-the-spot stomping of feet accompanied by cries from the thousands and thousands of fans begging for 'More! More! More!' enveloping the whole stadium, Bono sang one last number, a truly great version of 'Gloria', belting it out as he stood there almost drowning in his own sweat.

At the end, U2 finally said their goodbyes to America and left the stage, but not before Bono had pledged vows of a hasty return.

Bono was looking at me, laughing and grinning, reminding me of yesterday's prank with the car that they had bought.

'What happened to it?' I asked.

Still laughing, he said that John abandoned it somewhere between the Tri-State Bridge and Brendon Byrne Stadium, then hitched himself a ride as he had spent his last $200 on buying the car. Bono was really having fun, pausing in between telling me the story to roar with laughter. Apparently the car kept stopping and starting and sounded like it was about to blow up. It was at that stage that John made his wise decision to abort the journey.

Bono then joked that he was going to knock John for the $200 car money, and the thought of it now made him double up with laughter. After finally exhausting the fine details of yesterday's adventure, he came and stood right in front of me, as if to restrict my movement. Then, smiling, he placed his hands on either side of my shoulders, saying he had something he wanted to ask me.

'Get on with it then. What do you want?' I joked, smiling back at him, encouraging him to spit it out as I had a flight to catch.

'Well, that's just it,' he said, 'I was hoping that you would agree to come on to Dublin before you flew back home.' He asked me if I could accompany him and the other three band members back to Dublin instead of taking a direct flight home to London. The fact of the matter was that Bono wanted to discuss his plans around the art direction and costumes for the second leg of the tour. With a number of high-profile commitments already lined up back in Ireland, he had wanted me to help organise his outfits.

It would be a great time, so Bono thought, to be briefed about photographers seeking to capture the band's image on film – something that he had now started to take a keen interest in. It was going to be the perfect environment for talking and throwing ideas around without being interrupted, he said, adding, 'I will be relaxed, with nobody needing my time every minute of the waking day. Come on.' He winked at me, trying hard to manipulate my reply, throwing in the promise that he would take me to a pub where they served Guinness the like of which I would not taste anywhere else in the world.

I agreed, although it had nothing to do with the Guinness. I had my own agenda, thinking that, although it wasn't my style to explain or complain, the treatment being dealt to me by his management was finally taking its toll, and this would be an appropriate time to discuss my disillusionment.

'Good. Can you inform Ellen, and get her to alter your flight details?' he said.

'Actually, Bono, do you think you can inform her?' I answered sweetly.

Chapter 10

Dublin Fair City

It was certainly different, but I wasn't sure that I could have lived in such a cramped space, although the old Martello tower where Bono and his wife Ali lived had (as the estate agents would say) magnificent views of the Irish Sea. The outlying pastures were home to some of Ireland's finest beef, or perhaps they were dairy, cows. Co. Wicklow was a fine setting.

Spending a few days at Bono's home not only gave me time in which to discuss both the next phase of the tour with respect to clothes and art direction and the *Rattle and Hum* film, but also presented an opportunity – at the suggestion of both Ali and Bono – to clear out his wardrobe.

Using the same method that I had with the tour wardrobe trunks, I emptied the wardrobes of their possessions, placing the contents across his bed. Ali offered to be my assistant, overseeing from the side of the small bedroom where she had seated herself. With an approving eye, she offered her own thoughts and ideas about different pieces of clothing and the piles that they should eventually land up in – one was for keeping, the other for disposing – complimenting me occasionally when she thought I had made a good choice.

As we worked and chatted, Bono entered the room with outstretched hands offering us each a cup of tea. He said he had made it with love, but added that secretly it was his admission price for gaining entry into the room where the damage was being done. On spotting an old jumper, much the worse for wear, on one of the redundant piles he rescued it, saying that it had a lot of sentimental value.

Ali and Bono had an interesting idea to put forward. They felt that it would be a great help to them if I could finish the job by placing his clothes back into the closet in such a way that he could easily identify which items should be worn together, i.e. a pair of trousers would be teamed with a choice of shirt or tee shirt, and put on the same hanger. On the floor beneath would be my choice of footwear. I also teamed accessories like scarves, kerchiefs and hats, even selecting pieces of jewellery to finish off my selection, which I placed in the appropriate pockets.

Finally, I hand-printed on tags my choice of clothes for particular events. So on one tag I might write 'casual' or 'formal' then the tag would be hung on the neck of the appropriate hanger.

Still, I expressed my reservations about following such a procedure, assuring Bono that, as he now knew considerably more about the subtleties of creating an image, he was quite capable of dressing himself. I thought perhaps he was taking this whole image business to extremes.

He answered by saying it gave him a lot more confidence having his outfits selected for him, especially if he was attending some stylish function, adding that it gave him one less thing to think about, although he had no problem thinking about the next leg of the tour which was to kick off in two weeks' time, starting in Italy on 27 May 1987.

Our various discussions took place in his tiny white, stuccoed kitchen, as we sat around the table sipping tea. Here, he would express his feelings about the band, its history and his plans for it. He felt that the most important part of the band's career had been achieved. This occurred when he and U2 successfully conquered 'The Americas' with the first leg of the *Joshua Tree* tour. The real mark of their breakthrough was to be written up on the cover of *Time* magazine as 'The Hottest Ticket in Town', leaving the Yanks gagging for more.

I was interested to learn from Bono exactly how he was now feeling and thinking. I had detected a difference in him already since the start of the tour, feeling he was now more shut down – introverted. When I mentioned this to him, he agreed, and said that it was an astute observation. The more Bono gave of himself on stage, the more he kept for himself off stage.

And the more conscious I became of the change in Bono's personality, the more I wanted his image to progress in another direction – at least in terms of his look offstage. I was keen to play up his newfound ego. I wanted his style of dress to represent everything that he had now become, which I felt was more worldly and confident, yet at the same time raw and vulnerable.

Having seen Bono so often with a pen and pad in his hand, he appeared to me to be a cross between some pugnacious type of character and a poet, often appearing deep in thought. It was around this that I would start to develop ideas for his new image.

In crafting Bono's new look I was keen to play up his rawness, and was developing in my mind the idea of him as an artistic/warrior character. I was also reminded of one of our conversations where he revealed to me that he no longer wanted to project to his army of fans that he was accessible. This I felt was significant. He had given me the key.

His image, off stage at least, was going to be one of toughness; yet sophistication would have a role to play, which I knew Bono could now comfortably pull off.

Although Bono's character was to project strength, he still had to maintain a certain amount of vulnerability.

This I was hoping to achieve by using different fabrics. I was going to start introducing textures such as velvet into his wardrobe, along with a hint of colour. I felt that a warm-coloured wine velvet jacket – which I had already eyed on a previous shopping trip – teamed with a pair of jeans or even his beat-up leather trousers could definitely assist in projecting the poet side of his character, while also enhancing his rock'n'roll strength. It was a contradiction. But so was he.

We also decided that I would have a three-piece pin-striped suit tailored for him by the craftsmen of Italy, where we were soon to be. It would borrow from the style of the 1930s Al Capone gangsters. I was hoping to achieve a rugged, macho, bad-boy image, only I would team the look with colourful kerchiefs and loosely knotted ties, because I knew that Bono would give the look a bit of a twist and make it more rock'n'roll. I could see it making him look very sexy and sophisticated.

Once we'd developed a clear understanding of where I was taking them in terms of their visual image, I now wanted to broach the subject of Ellen and Principal Management with Bono. I certainly did not want to sound like a telltale tit, but I was fucked off and, although I loved my job, I abhorred the constant apprehension that surrounded it.

Bono suggested that he travel back into Dublin to the Shelbourne Hotel with me (where I was now booked in to spend the next few nights, having promised to party with some friends who were flying over from London to meet up). It was in the back of the car travelling from Co. Wicklow to Dublin that I finally brought up the subject (or subjects) of my discontent.

Bono said that he was not at all surprised to hear what I had told him, although he was surprised, so he said, that I was so green to the world of rock'n'roll. 'Lola,' he said, 'this is what it's like. Welcome aboard to the devil and rock'n'roll!' He then took hold of my hand and said, 'You are working for me and what I think about you is all that matters.'

I did not agree or feel at all comforted, and questioned myself for having ever mentioned it.

Bono then enquired about the fashion and photographic industry, which was my background. 'Isn't that filled with the same problems?' he asked. I laughed. Nothing I'd known, and believe me I did not fall out of the sky, had a patch on the rock scene.

I insisted to Bono that he redefine my job description, which at that point was wardrobe director. I believed that would help to dispel a lot of bad feeling from Ellen and Principal Management. I explained to him that I did not like the rumours being put out about me.

But Bono did not let me finish. Interrupting, he said he did not give a fuck what any one of his staff felt and mentioned that jealousy was rife in the industry, advising me that I would have to toughen up to deal with it. I once again protested, and asked him to at least explain to Ellen and Paul McGuiness why he had hired me, adding that I would like it if he told them what our daily meetings were about. He said that he would, and added that he was completely happy with my work and what I had already achieved for the band. 'Lola, you are working for me and you have my entire backing,' he assured me as he bid me farewell, telling me to make the most of my time with my friends. 'You'll be back to work pretty soon. Don't worry about a thing.' He winked as he made his way to the bar of the Shelbourne Hotel where some of his friends were waiting.

Chapter 11

The Comforts of Home

It was a little disorientating waking up in my own bed, after all the different hotel rooms. I lay there for a while, acclimatising myself to the noises outside the bedroom window. There was a lot to get used to. The awful sound of the dustbin truck's alarm as it reversed itself down the last of the cobbled London streets alerting all and sundry to its presence; the screaming of a mother to her youngster, warning the child of the dangers of running out into the road. As if her screeching tones were not enough, she must have smacked the child, as it began wailing and sobbing. But it was the distant sound of a dog barking that was my cue to leave my bed for the kitchen and some coffee.

I had almost a fortnight to play around in London and catch up with some of my good friends. As I sat there sipping at my coffee, I decided not to waste a moment more and began to phone around inviting some people over for supper.

Everything felt so surreal as I walked around Soho making my way towards Brewer Street market and my favourite Italian deli. It had been less than two months since I was last home. Touring with the most talked-about band in the world made everyday life seem mundane, although, when I was on the road, I constantly yearned for the normality of the everyday.

I was determined that I was going to cook up a feast for the friends I had invited to dine with me and no expense was spared for the banquet. Finishing my grocery shopping inside Patisserie Valerie on Old Compton Street, I relaxed, taking tea and sampling a cream cake before I made any major decisions about the delights I would present to my dinner guests. Eventually, after making my pastry purchases, I left the shop, stepped back on to the street and hailed a passing taxi to take me and my heavy load of groceries back to Camden Town.

Mark had turned up early and I was so happy to see him, not only because his taste in music was impeccable, but also because he was one of my closest friends and we had hung out together for years. I had missed his charm and wit. He was not inside the flat for a minute before he had the tunes on, and was 'billin it', happily chatting away filling me in with all the latest gossip.

As the bell to my flat didn't work and I had never

bothered to fix it, not wanting the local toe-rags to be able to keep ringing it (the norm in my neighbourhood), I had asked Mark to listen out for the sound of a pebble tapping against the window, as this was the method used for my friends in the know to gain entry.

My guests had arrived and we were all sitting around getting nicely stoned, chilling out, just listening to sounds that Mark had kept us supplied with. Ronnie was getting hungry and demanded that we now sit around the table to eat as she headed in the direction of the kitchen, beckoning me to assistant with the pasta (well, it was my type of banquet). Trisha requested that Mark play something a little more chilled while we ate.

With all our hugs, greetings and news now out of the way, Ronnie wasted no time in asking the question that was uppermost in her mind. 'So, Lola, who's got the biggest dick – Bono, Larry, Adam or Edge?'

A little taken aback at the question, though knowing my friends I should not have been, I held them in suspense for a few moments, allowing time for the laughter to die down. Then, in a teasing tone, I told them how bloody common I thought they were. More laughter and jesting about U2's body parts. Now everybody was speaking at once. And I was told to answer the question. In a tone of voice now feigning disgust, I said that was 'private information', but I couldn't help laughing at the thought of it, eventually saying, 'But it isn't Bono.' Once more, the sound of laughter around the table.

'You're going to have to tell us,' insisted Peter. 'I have a friend who's dying to know everything you have to reveal about U2. He absolutely loves them. Especially Larry.'

'Oh, oh,' I interrupted excitedly, waving my hands about, eager to tell the sex-shop story about how I had purchased a pair of leather chaps for Larry from the famous LA store without giving any thought to his macho image. 'Remind me to tell you the story that happened with him.'

'Tell us. Come on,' Peter urged me. 'We can't have our best mate working with U2 and not reveal all.'

And this is how my dinner party proceeded. And, like all good dinner parties, the entire evening was spent discussing sex, drugs, and rock'n'roll – along with the tiniest details of my work, which my friends took a keen interest in, wanting to know about everything from which famous celebrities I had met and what happened backstage at a gig (especially in the band's dressing room) to what brand of pants Bono wore. One would never have guessed that this group of people held such high-profile jobs, working alongside some very famous celebrities themselves.

'Are you enjoying it? And are you happy? That what's important,' Ronnie said.

So I proceeded to purge myself of my angst over Ellen Darst, recounting the whole sorry tale to everyone around the table. I said, 'It's as if we both come from different planets.'

I continued telling them how, from my very first

meeting, Ellen and I had rubbed each other up the wrong way. 'I mean, I had no dealings with her. How could I possibly have offended her?' I asked, hoping they could throw some light on the matter.

Mark replied, 'It's that haughty look of yours. You know the one, where you look down that big nose of yours, like you're judging us all.'

'So what you're saying, Mark, is I should have a nose job to please her?'

Once again we were all laughing.

With a little help from the grass we were smoking, we all became quite intense and concerned by my dilemma, with everybody chipping in with their suggestions.

As a Marvin Gaye CD played away in the background, I carried on telling them all about the clashes between Ellen and me. 'Girl, they don't know you,' Trisha said sarcastically, laughing. 'You're like a little lap dog. Anybody's nice to you, you roll over.'

'Yeah,' I answered, not quite taking on board what she said. 'Seriously, it's been scary.'

'Do you know,' I continued, 'she has actually warned me my days are numbered.'

'Oh fuck her,' shouted Peter, pouring himself some more wine from the other end of the table. 'Tell her to stick the job up her big fat American backside.'

'No way,' Ronnie said. 'You show the fuckers what you're made of. There's no way that you should let that bitch mess with you.'

'I know but it becomes so difficult.' I explained to them that I not only had my day-to-day work cut out for me, but that I was also constantly on my guard as to what would be thrown at me next.

I looked around the table at my friends, hoping they would be able to share their thoughts on my next question, which was, 'How do I try to make friends with the crew when they all appear to be in her camp?' I quickly added, 'Don't you dare say I'm paranoid. She has actually told me.'

I then reiterated what Ellen had said to me once, which was, did I think I could take on her and all of her staff?

At this point Peter said jokingly that I should end the story as I was spooking him. 'How did you sleep at night?' he enquired.

Everyone else spoke in unison saying, 'How the fuck did she sleep at night?'

There was no stopping me by this stage. It was like I needed to cleanse myself, and felt rather fortunate to have the interest of my close friends. Going a step further, I told them of various other incidents that had taken place.

One such story concerned a daily work requirement of mine, which I mentioned was not exclusive to me but other people who worked with the band as well as band members. I explained that, when bands of U2's calibre are out on the road touring, chauffeur-driven cars were a normal part of the job. Further, I was disorientated by the fact that every few days would see me in a different

American state, and I needed to shop with very little knowledge of each town's layout. Time also being of the essence, a car and driver became a necessity.

Each day, I continued, I would touch base with Theresa, the tour travel co-ordinator, requesting my daily transport requirements. I would tell her what time I would need a vehicle and driver and so on. She would then proceed to execute my request, each time ordering me a limousine. And each time I would thank her but suggest that next time a small town car would be more suitable.

I explained that these conversations between us had become standard. And, even though I would point out to her the fact that a smaller car would be a lot less expensive, not to mention inconspicuous, one was never made available to me. This pissed me off, especially as a lot of the time I would be shopping around in vintage second-hand stores, trying hard to source some unusual item of clothing for a relatively good price, being forever conscious that I was trying to balance my allocated budget, as well as keep Bob Koch off my back. Stepping out of a limousine, I felt, somewhat hindered my chances.

I then explained the reverse psychology ploy I had used. Even though it had worked in theory, as having made the request for a limousine I finally got a small town car, it had been reported back to Ellen that I had demanded a limo.

I went on to give them yet another example, informing my friends that even the tour accountant was making my life difficult, interrogating me over the fact he could not see how I could possibly be spending so much money on Bono and the other band members' clothes. And I retold the Paul McGuiness and Ellen Darst saga, where I was warned not to believe I was indispensable.

I ended by relating how Ellen and Paul had the cheek to tell me that I would have to pay the Boston hotel's room expenses, even though Bono had ordered the room service and emptied my room's mini-bar of booze.

'So why the fuck didn't you just say that to that McGuiness bloke? For goodness sake, Lola,' Trisha sighed.

At this point Peter interjected. 'Yeah, well, I see what that accountant geezer means about spending so much money on their clothes. You have to admit, how much money does it cost to dress them in torn-up jeans and old tee shirts? They always look so scruffy to me.'

'Thanks, Pete,' I said sarcastically, then laughed, slightly amused as I went into a speech about the difficulties I had trying to create for Bono and U2 a raw-looking image – one which would appear uncontrived and natural, even though a lot of hard work, thought and money had gone into it. Then I continued to bore them with explanations about the use of fabrics, telling them that it was essential to use more expensive material, and that I had sourced many fabrics to have a lot of the clothes tailored in. Cloth that was able to stand the test of time, I said. Fabrics that were able to survive friction, heat and dampness caused by sweat from being on stage and in the spotlight. I finished off by adding that I had some of Bono's Levi jeans and trousers reworked or specially made up to look like regular pairs.

They all had been listening attentively, now wanting to know exactly what Bono's thoughts were about the clashes with his management.

'Well, I didn't exactly break things down,' I said. 'I felt uncomfortable having to mention any of it. It all sounds so juvenile, don't you think?'

'Mark, can you please put on a more uplifting CD?' Ronnie implored.

With all the love and support of my friends I felt better, and more importantly felt that I could and would continue with the *Joshua Tree* tour, although a feeling of foreboding had stayed with me, one that was like the nagging of a toothache.

If it wasn't taken care of, it would cause more discomfort – even pain.

Chapter 12

Stars in his Eyes

Peter had stayed the night and I was woken up next morning by the sounds of revelry as I heard Peter and Jalle, another friend of ours, screaming with laughter. Curious to find out what all the fuss was about, I went to investigate.

Standing in the hallway of my apartment was Peter, dressed head to toe in Bono's jeans and boots which were sizes too big for him, even though he had belted the jeans and completed the impersonation by donning Bono's cowboy hat. He was ignoring my screams of shocked horror, as I yelled, 'I don't believe it,' ordering him to get out of the clothes, and asking him what on earth he was doing going into my luggage. But he took not the slightest notice and kept on mincing and parading about the flat as he attempted to sing 'With or Without You'.

I too had to crease up with laughter. Seeing my gay friend, who was tall and handsome, with a lean, lithe body that was toned and fit, running up and down the flat on the tips of his toes, pretending to be Bono and demanding that I do lewd things to him, was hilarious, even though I told him to shut up, and demanded once again that he get out of Bono's clothes.

Jalle was hysterical, and in between fits of laughter said, 'I bet Bono wishes he had a body like yours, Pete,' to which Peter replied that he wished he had Bono's money.

Peter had agreed to wait in at my flat in order to take possession of some clothes that I was having biked across the band, from the boutique Browns, on South Molton Street, in London's West End. They were a selection of very expensive leather jackets, designer trousers and various sweaters, shirts and suits.

After reminding Peter to listen out for the bike, having informed the courier company that my doorbell was out of order, I left the flat. Peter called out to me asking if it was OK to stay a few nights more. I shouted back that it was cool.

My time in London was spent visiting family and partying with friends and, as most of my friends were involved in some way or another with my line of business, this meant I was forever working.

Catherine Dyer, now Mrs David Bailey, was an up-and-coming model. Peter and Les were choreographers (to some famous rock stars themselves) and absolutely brilliant dancers. Then there was John Moore, who was the hunkiest cordwainer you ever set eyes on (and is sadly no longer with us). He would eventually make boots and shoes for Bono. Ronnie was the tip-top beauty therapist to the stars, and spent a lot of her time kneading their bodies and mopping their brows (when she wasn't putting up with me begging her for a massage). Trisha was a stylist more involved with films and commercials. Lizzie Tear was an up-and-coming singer, and at the time was dating the Hayzee Fantayzee singer, now DJ, Jeremy Healy. They lived across the street from me, and near some other neighbourhood friends, Jeffrey Hinton and Princess Julia, who had also made it on the DJ scene. Jalle was a make-up artist. Michael Enns was a silk-screen artist and worked for Andy Warhol in his New York studio The Factory. He was also a photographer and I happened to have fallen madly in love with him, which was why he was about to arrive in London. And then there was Abe Hamilton. Abe was not only a very talented fashion designer, but also one of my closet friends whose talent I respected. And, though all of his amazing clothes were designed for women, he was to introduce me to and educate me on the merits of different fabrics and materials. I used his suggestions for some of the items of clothing I had made up for Bono.

My friends were party animals, so most of my work was

done inside the popular clubs and bars of London, where we would often exchange ideas.

My flat was an old 1930s-style mansion block set in a part of London known as Somers Town. This neighbourhood is on the borders of Camden Town and Euston. The small flat that I owned was sandwiched between a Peabody trust house and some old boozer.

Looking at the old mansion block from the outside, no one would guess that the interior of my apartment was renovated in a very modern style, whilst a lot of the original interior 1930s features remained untouched. One of these was a Victorian-style picture rail that ran the length of the hallway.

This rail was often used for hanging the clothes that had overflowed from the dress rails of my studio. This left the hallway full of designer clothes dangling from hangers placed over the lipping of the frame.

On this particular day in May 1987, it was packed to capacity, not only holding the clothes that Browns had ferried across, but also heavily laden with some old leather biker jackets that I had managed to source, at Bono's request, from a shop on the King's Road in Chelsea.

That day provided quite a coup. Not only had I found the leather jackets – one of which had some very distinct markings on its back – but I had purchased the 'American Inca' shirt jacket that was eventually worn by Edge – as seen on the frequently used image for the *Rattle and Hum* film and album cover.

It had been fun spending time with Peter, and I used to joke with him that he could make his fortune packaging himself as the panacea to manic depression. He was such a funny bastard, but also the biggest liberty-taker in the world, as I was about to discover.

In between flitting around town, I also had to spend a good deal of time on the phone, making future appointments as well as interacting constantly with Principal Management, who would notify me almost daily of any messages or requests from Larry, Adam, Bono or Edge. I too would keep them loosely informed of my activities.

And on this particular day, I happened to mention the fantastic leather Harley biker jacket that I had bought for Bono. I went into great detail about the design on the back of it, explaining that the silver studded outline of an eagle etched on it was the only one of its kind. All this I had patiently explained to Judy who was the wife of a member of the crew.

You can imagine my alarm when, at 10pm, while relaxing at home with a quiet drink and a bit of TV, the phone suddenly rang. It was Judy, screaming down the phone over the loud music that was playing in the venue she was calling from. She was telling me that my home must have been burgled because there was this skinny guy inside the club dancing and throwing himself about the dance floor with Bono's jacket on. It has to be the one, she said, as it had markings identical to those I had described earlier.

'Hmm,' I said to myself, repeating back to Judy, 'Skinny, was he?'

'Yes,' she replied.

'Good dancer?' I asked.

'Yeah real amazing,' she said.

'Tall and handsome?'

'Gorgeous,' she said, laughing as she remarked that if one was going to have a burglary, they should all look like him.

'Grab the fucking bastard,' I said. 'It's my flatmate Peter.' I encouraged her to confront him and bring him to the phone, but Judy was not feeling confident enough, so she said, to execute such an order. So instead I ordered a taxi, quickly dressed myself and headed into Soho.

I made the cab wait while I rushed inside to check if Peter or Judy were still there, but they had obviously moved on. Having my suspicions about where Peter might end up that night, I asked the driver to take me on to Charing Cross, where the gay club Heaven was.

Without any shame, I marched in to the middle of the dance floor, having spotted Peter and the jacket with a group of friends all mashing it up to the music. I went straight over to where he was dancing and, now standing directly in front of him so he couldn't move, I let forth a string of expletives.

If I could have reached one of his earlobes I would have grabbed it and frogmarched him off the dance floor. Instead I returned to my East End roots, and started screaming and shouting and throwing my arms about to fully express the point of my fury, telling him in no uncertain terms exactly what I thought of him. We both left the club very quickly to discuss the matter at home. Peter's reply to my scolding was that he felt he was doing me a favour and that wasn't the way I should be repaying him.

'I don't know what you mean,' I replied.

'Well, girl,' he said, 'I'm saving you the trouble of having the jacket tied up to the back of some old truck in the hope of giving it a more lived-in effect. Instead I'm wearing it to achieve the more authentic worn-out version that you seem to like so much.' (Peter was referring to an incident that was reported in the tabloids where I had a leather jacket of Bono's tied to the back of a truck.) Reassuring me, Peter said Bono would appreciate his efforts.

Now it all made sense to me – why Peter had been so keen on staying over at my flat. He had planned to use Bono's clothes as his clubbing drag.

I never dared to tell Bono that my gay friend had been camping about London town in his clothes. Although an amused smile did cross my face every time I saw Bono dressed in the jacket.

Chapter 13

From the Backroom
of the Infamous

For some unknown reason I could not get to sleep. I just lay awake in an almost hypnotised state, listening to Michael's rhythmic snores and wondering why the sake that I'd consumed earlier hadn't rendered me unconscious. Maybe I was excited about leaving to go back out on the road again, or so I told myself, as I tried breathing deeply in through my nose and out through my mouth like they teach you in yoga. But I could not stop the thoughts that had started to drift into my mind, and which, for some unknown reason, centred around my childhood.

Darting somewhere else now, like thoughts do, I had a realisation that it was almost a year since my dad had died, on 17 April 1986.

Sleep would not come and I now no longer fought it, I just lay there warmed by the heat of Michael's body, indulging my subconscious. I started thinking about my strange bohemian upbringing.

Well, it certainly wasn't normal. It always felt slightly strange when, as I was growing up, living in the East End of London, other friends had parents who took them to play in the park on the weekends and had lunches at Wimpy. Sometimes they even went to a movie. What must that have been like? I had often wondered, now trying hard to conjure up an image of my dad in a park.

Regressing further back, with my mind full of thoughts about my dad, I thought about how the nearest I got to green fields with him was at the gee-gees or at Hackney Wick dog track on a Saturday morning. I remembered vividly now the smells and noises, even the faces of some very peculiar-looking men with even stranger-sounding names, like Kiki and One-arm Lou. Back then, I was curious to know why some men wore white gloves and waved their hands about in the air, tapping their heads or their noses. Whatever they were doing, I thought it very odd and told my dad. I remembered how he laughed that warm laugh of his, as he knelt down to level with a nine-year-old and explain that those men were tick-tacking the odds. I was none the wiser.

If I had been very good, my dad would say – but what he meant was if he had a win – I would be allowed to have a late night and, along with my other siblings, who were my older brother Martin and my sister Karen, go to Walthamstow dog track. My other sister Rochelle could not come because she was too young.

This I thought was the real thing, sitting at a window table that allowed clear vision of the dogs racing, swinging my feet beneath the table, as I munched away on my chips with not a care in the world.

The thought right now of not having a care in the world felt alien.

This was dad's way, I supposed, of bonding with his kids. I screwed my face into a smirk, amused.

Tossing and turning, I had now disturbed Michael, who wanted to know if I was all right. I touched his leg with my leg to confirm my safety, not wanting to talk so that I would remain in my mind and at the dog track. I had now equated the smells, noise and bustling ambience of the Saturday morning races, with a night out at a U2 gig.

I missed my dad, and a sad feeling had started to engulf me. I imagined what he would say about a man like Paul McGuiness. This thought amused me, knowing he would have him down as a mug, albeit a rich one. I guess most people think their parents are cool, but I really was inspired by my dad. He didn't care whether I stayed on at school or travelled the world. In fact, he had even encouraged me to travel, saying, 'Travel the world. Experience different countries and cultures. Learn new languages. And, Lola ...' – he would say my name to emphasise the point – '... listen to what other people have to say.' He added that I should never underestimate anybody. This was his advice to me, believing that travel was the best education anyone could ever get. I did not need much coaxing to leave school. I abhorred being stuck inside the same place day after day.

I remember, from a very early age, Dad lining me and my sister up, and announcing to us that 'There's no such thing as a nice Jewish boy, so go travel the world.' It was not hard to think he was nuts, with his ideology and filthy temper.

Travel was very shortly to be high on my list of things to do, having been invited by my best friend Yvonne Lamont-Campbell's boss Maureen to join her and Yvonne on a week's trip to Greece. We were so excited. Yvonne and I had plotted together for a week, thinking up stories to tell my dad, hoping that he would allow me to go. My dad was a bit overprotective and usually never even allowed me to sleep over at friends' houses, but he had no problem with my friends staying over at our home.

Maureen's hairdresser's was sandwiched between the Black Boy public house, and the Stepney Green steam baths that my dad and his mates used weekly for a day of *schvitzing*. Here they would spend most of the day relaxing in the steam, as well as eating and gambling – playing a card game known as Kalooki.

Yvonne had held her weekend job for some time at the salon and this we felt would be our bargaining chip, hopefully making Dad more lenient. He adored Yvonne and knew of her place of work. Between the two of us, we did eventually manage to wear him down and, after he had spoken with Maureen, he agreed that I could go.

Maureen was the typical Essex wife – before there ever *were* Essex wives – and, with us being teenagers, she was, I guess, what Yvonne and I secretly aspired to be. With her straight bleached blonde hair and immaculately painted nails and face, she always appeared so worldly and feminine. Jimmy, her boyfriend, would come and collect her most evenings from work, turning up in a series of flashy cars. When he saw me in the saloon, he would always stop and ask after my old man, telling me to pass on his regards. Jimmy was another one Dad had down as a mug.

It was a hot spring morning as we sat on the hotel veranda eating breakfast. We had been in Greece for two days, although we had not done much sunbathing – Maureen had been keen to shop. Yvonne and I did not want to appear ungrateful, as Maureen had treated us to the holiday, so we said nothing as she planned another day of spending.

The third morning, as we sat at our usual table to eat breakfast, and without any prior warning, we were suddenly surrounded by men, and frogmarched, screaming, from the hotel into separate cars, terrified, with absolutely no idea of who, what, why or where.

It was not long before I discovered these men were the police. What followed was like something out of *Midnight Express*: dark, dank dungeons; police interrogations; a complete lack of contact with each other or home; and all pleas for a lawyer ignored. I was almost raped, but managed to fight like a woman possessed to defend myself.

To say that I was afraid would not begin to describe the trauma, and only after a week of being without food and contact did I finally manage to remember and dial my home telephone number. That was when I broke the dreadful news to my father. He was by this stage already in contact with Interpol.

We were held accused of having counterfeit money. This was something Yvonne and I discovered much later on in the prison. Not having had a clue what was going on, it was alleged that Jimmy had asked Maureen to take a parcel for him to Greece, and explained to her that somebody would contact her and arrange to collect it. What he didn't know was that she would open the parcel and allegedly use some of the American dollars from it, hence the non-stop shopping trips.

No parcel was ever found, but one of the stores had notified the police on discovering that the dollars Maureen had supposedly used were counterfeit and, as we were part of her party, we were also accused.

It took my father almost three months of battling with the Greek authorities to secure our bail, after which Yvonne and I were eventually ferried safely back to England.

I never heard from Maureen again, and nobody was to ever see or hear of Jimmy either.

Now, as I began to doze, my thoughts suddenly turned in an entirely different direction: bringing images of Dad and his input with my homework. How that man used to annoy me. He had the ability to associate everything with gambling – from recreational pastimes to school homework, and it would irritate me.

His way of helping me with my maths schoolwork was to teach me to break down betting equations, which he felt would help me have a better understanding of fractions and times tables. How on earth he managed to make four-legged creatures the focus of my English essays I'll never know, but he did. As for board games like Monopoly, forget it. They never stood a chance in our house against a game of cards or a dice. Oh he was so cool, my dad. Smiling to myself, I thought that if there had been a gaming academy he would have enrolled me. I gave a little laugh curled up in my bed, cuddling at Michael now for safety, thinking that it would be some achievement, graduating with an honours degree in the shuffling of cards, or even the game of craps.

'Come on, sleep,' I told myself. 'You're almost hallucinating.' But still sleep didn't come.

My father was an infamous East End character and was known as 'The Boot' (his nose resembled the map of Italy). This was caused by a pugnacious night out when he was a youth.

It was in the backroom of his illegal drinking and gaming clubs that I was to experience my first taste of work. In the smoky, dank atmosphere of the card room, I would go about table from table, taking orders for teas and sandwiches from his mates, who also happened to be some of England's most notorious criminals.

Not that I was ever aware of some of the notoriety of these 'faces'. They were always dressed immaculately in what appeared like uniforms of crisp white shirts and suits. Their ties would sometimes be pulled loosely from around their necks, and the cuffs of their shirts were always matched with expensive-looking cufflinks that glittered every time the table light reflected the diamonds or rubies mounted in them. When a player rolled up his shirtsleeve, with nicotine-stained fingers that always bore a ring of sorts, you would invariably spot a silver armband.

The beautifully tailored mohair or silk suits would usually always have their jackets draped carefully over the backs of chairs, some personalised with a hankie poking out from the top of the breast pocket. The belts and braces also lent a personalised signature to the various rogues' attire, adding a certain elegant appeal to the men, almost like they were city bankers, I thought. It really made a lasting impression on me, the way these characters dressed, with no detail ever overlooked.

Life's a funny old thing, I was thinking to myself. You take a typical powerbroker, with their university educations, and then compare them with those notorious criminals who used to gamble around the card table what is the difference between them. One sits behind a desk, the other behind a card table.

Although I have to say that the villains around the card table always tipped me, as well as affording me the utmost respect. It was hard to believe they were capable of some of their crimes.

Chapter 14

Back on the Road

O nce again I was packing bags, ready to hit the road. And as usual, I was laden down with luggage. There were not only the new purchases but a lot of the band's older items of clothing, which I had brought back home to get them restyled and altered, and in some cases copied. They all needed to be packed. And as I looked around at all the cases, including my own luggage, I got the distinct feeling that the flat now resembled a luggage hold.

There was just enough time for a final farewell supper with my mates, only this time we would all meet at the Kensington Hilton Hotel for a Japanese meal. This dinner party, although serving a different flavour of food and drink, which we were downing like the sake was about to dry up, had a very similar tone to our last evening spent together, with every one of my friends ever keen to glean tales of U2.

I had had enough. 'I'm bored,' I told them as they all sat around the table bombarding me with questions about U2. 'If I didn't know you all better, I'd think you just wanted to hang out with me so that we can speak about Larry, Adam, Edge and Bono.'

The sarcasm continued, with Mark saying, 'Why else would we dine with you twice in a fortnight?'

'Oh come on, girl,' Pete said. 'All we want to know is who's shagging who.'

'And you haven't told us if they do drugs,' Trisha added.

'Give me a break. Get a life,' I told them. 'Hey, you guys are beginning to worry me. What is it that makes you so interested in them?' I looked at each of them around the table. 'What did we all used to talk about before?'

'Quick, get the waiter's attention,' I said to Michael, wanting to order some more sake. 'Come on. What is it about them that's so special?'

Each one had an answer but they all spoke at once and, in between downing their beers and sakes, voiced their opinions, which were basically the same. U2 were the most talked-about band of the time, generating so much hype and interest that even my friends had caught the bug.

Even though I made my feelings clear, they kept insisting that I at least answer their questions, which were continually repeated while I was eating my sushi. Trisha was relentless in her quest to find out if the band did drugs. By this time she had aroused the rest of the group's curiosity on the subject, and they all wanted an answer. 'Did Bono do drugs?'

'Oh, Lola. What are you being so secretive about?' Michael asked impatiently, challenging me almost. 'We're your closest friends.'

'Lola, are they these God-fearing Christians that we are led to believe?' Trisha now had found another question she wanted an answer to.

I finally replied by telling them that I personally had never done drugs with Bono. 'Well, so far, but give me time,' I joked.

I then told them my thoughts about Bono and drugs. To me, he seemed like the type of person who would check out everything at least once, but I stressed the fact that I had never witnessed him taking drugs. Although I had been privy to some of his heavy boozing sessions, I said, laughing, 'Boy, can they get out of control.'

'Well thank fuck for that,' Peter said. 'Because he bores me with his sanctimonious ramblings. At least the booze makes me feel like he really is a rock'n'roller.'

'And what about the others?' Mark butted in.

'Yeah, that one who always wears a hat. What's his name?' Trisha wanted to know.

'Edge,' I answered. 'Well, I did get stoned at a party with his ex-wife, but got called away before I actually witnessed Edge inhaling.'

'Fuck, Lol. Can't you just answer the question? Do they do drugs, yes or no?'

An argument now broke out between Michael and me, with me telling him that there was not a direct answer, and I was doing my best to answer as accurately as I could.

'Go on, Lola,' Mark said, before turning to Michael, half-teasing him by saying he was to shut his big American gob. 'Let Lola answer the questions in her own way.'

'Well, I can tell you categorically,' I said, now looking directly at Michael, proving that I could answer a direct question, 'that, out of all of them, Adam is the party animal. And I know because I have partied with him.' I went on to say that I had stayed over at his house when I was in Ireland.

I also went in to some details about the impression that the band had on me, explaining to them that as far as I was concerned Adam was the odd one out. With no relationship happening, he was the only single member of the band, and he did not seem to get on with Bono, Larry or Edge, spending very little time off stage with any of them. But, I added, he was close to U2's manager Paul McGuiness.

'Oh, that's why you don't like him much,' Michael said, knowing my own very private views on McGuiness.

'Well, now you mention it ...' I replied sarcastically, 'but, no, actually it really has nothing to do with that. He's just wet. I can't explain him. He has no personality, and I'm finding it very difficult to dress him. It's something I can't quite put my finger on.'

My guests were all now laughing and jesting, as they finished their food and ordered more drinks. I could see Trisha was keen for me to continue.

'Well, you see, because I don't know who he is, it makes my job a lot more difficult.'

'How do you mean?' Michael queried.

'Not knowing what to buy for him,' I replied. 'I have no idea how to dress him; who or what am I buying for.' I looked around the table, trying to prove a point. 'For me to make Adam look really cool, I would have to have him wear the clothes, and not the clothes wear him. And at this moment in time that is not happening.'

I finished by giving them an example of what I meant. 'I identify Bono with poet-like qualities, and even contradictory, warrior-type traits,' I said, 'so this allows me a lot of leverage when I am out sourcing his clothes. Look at any photo of U2 and you will see that Adam just doesn't look like he belongs. He sticks out like a sore thumb.'

'Well, why not buy him Ivy League kind of clothes, because he reminds me of those college geeks. Don't you think so?' Trisha interjected, laughing.

There was no letting up, and in between the downing of beers and sakes my friends were relentless with their questions, occasionally allowing some lewd remark to filter into the conversation, which would see the table erupt with laughter.

Finally having sated their curiosity (for the time being anyway), and having fully satisfied them that U2 were not the clean-living, Christian, holier-than-thou rock band their press office would have us all believe, but were four fragile human beings, very capable of succumbing to earthly vices, we were ready to go our separate ways.

I kissed and hugged each of my friends, and departed for home with Michael. Trisha and Peter insisted that they would meet up with me somewhere in Europe. I didn't hold my breath.

The next morning, Michael and I waited for the taxi to take us to Heathrow, where we would catch a flight to Dublin. Michael was excited, although he was trying to act cool. He had never been to Ireland before, so we planned to spend our last night together in the Shelbourne Hotel, with Michael then flying back home to the States the following morning. I had to begin work as soon as I arrived in Ireland, which left Michael to his own devices. But the evening was perfect, and very emotional as we said our farewells, unsure when we would see each other next.

The U2 machine then started to rock'n'roll, kicking off in Rome for the start of the second leg of the *Joshua Tree* tour, which was being staged across Europe. It was hard to believe that I'd been free of the backstage dressing rooms for a fortnight, as I was reunited with U2's flight trunks at the Stadio Flamino in Tiziano. I quickly got back into the routine, and began unpacking the boys' newly sourced clothes and preparing their dressing room and shower area, placing each band member's washrobes and toiletries about the sinks and showers. I checked in with the caterers, making sure Bono's specifically requested supplies of Jack Daniels were on hand, as well as touching base with Tom for the courtesy greetings. I didn't want to leave anything to chance.

I checked the band's stage clothes for wear and tear, brushing and shaking them free of dust and the creases that had now appeared (not only could I not sew, but my ironing left a lot to be desired). Then I selected the outfits for U2's first night back on stage.

This being Europe, the backstage guest list was expected to be long, with a lot of family, friends and celebrities flying in to catch the gigs.

I had no problem preparing Bono's clothes for the after-gig party. I had already spoken to him earlier in the day, and he had confided to me that he was beside himself ('totally freaked out and uncomfortable' were his exact words) about the ballooning of his weight, adding that I would have to help him do something about it.

As I was no dietician, I started with what I knew, and that was to dress him from head to toe in black, pulling from his wardrobe his favourite black shirt along with a pair of black trousers one size bigger than those he normally wore. These trousers were copies of his regular jeans, except I had them made a size larger in case of an emergency – like now. Black was Bono's comfort blanket and whenever he felt fat he would take to wearing it, in the hope that it made him appear slimmer.

There was a real buzz in the air backstage, with all the crew replenished from the fortnight's break. Laughter and greetings were everywhere, with the main talk between the men being of drugs and women, as the roadies told tales of their supposed nights of debauchery. Exchanging graphic descriptions as they spoke loudly among themselves, wanting to be overheard, they laughed and boasted of the beautiful girls they had 'laid', whose telephone numbers, one suspected, had only been obtained via idle promises of an introduction to Bono.

Although this was the first day back to work, there was to be no soundcheck. This, and the fact that they now they had the luxury of a privately hired Hawker Sidley 3B series to jet them about, allowed the band to fly out to Rome much later. We spent almost a week in Italy seeing them play at venues in Rome and Bologna. This meant we also had at least a few days free to shop and sightsee.

Bono, Larry and Edge were interested in seeing the Vatican, as was I. So Dennis Sheehan, U2's tour manager, organised a trip for us, together with Aisling – Edge's then wife – who had flown over with their young girls to spend some time on the road, in an attempt to repair their marriage. Larry's girlfriend, Anne, was also going to spend some time on the road with him.

With all of us packed like sardines inside a people-carrier, and not a limousine in sight, Bono joked about the difference between this and the way he and the band were treated in the States, where he felt like royalty. 'Welcome home to Europe,' he said. I grinned, thinking to myself that they should have let me organise the transport with Theresa.

We arrived at the dome to be informed by Dennis that we only had a limited amount of time to look around with a press lunch already arranged for Bono and the boys back at the Cavalieri Hilton Hotel. On hearing this, I decided I would break from the band and leg it around by myself, which would also allow me time, so I thought, to buy the holy water that I so wanted to take back home to Rose as a gift. She was my mother's friend and neighbour and also a devout Catholic.

I just managed to hear Dennis's voice as he shouted out after us all, just moments before we were about to step inside the building, calling out to no one in particular the precise time that he wanted us back at the car. He stood in the middle of Vatican City looking like an old schoolmaster, with his salt and pepper hair blowing all about his face, yelling out warnings to his pupils not to be late.

It seemed crazy attempting to see the inside of the Vatican with so little time, but I did my best, promising myself that I would come back one day with Michael. Time flew by, and I thought I'd better suss out the holy water situation. I soon realised that I would need something to put the water in, and was informed that you could buy these plastic, nun-shaped bottles from the Vatican gift shop. After doing so I was to follow the signs to the main building and, supposedly, the water.

The scale of the Vatican was so vast I started to accelerate the pace as I made for the shop, cursing myself for not having allowed enough time (although it was hardly the appropriate place for blaspheming). I spied Dennis who had also spotted me and was waving his hand, beckoning me towards him, as I was late. Ignoring him and keeping my head low, I continued on my mission, steaming into the gift shop panicking, thinking I might have to abandon my plan. Then Aisling dashed inside the shop, pleading with me to hurry. I started to explain to her that I had to have this holy water, by which time she had decided that she too had to get some, for her mother back in Ireland.

With our plastic nun water bottles purchased, we ran like madwomen, asking everybody where to get the holy water from. Nobody, it seemed, understood our English. Not stopping to hear their replies or read the signs on the walls indicating the direction for the water, we continued running around like headless chickens, with Edge now hot on our heels – sent to muster us up by Dennis – while Bono, Larry and the rest of the party sat impatiently waiting in the car.

By this time I had spotted a purple and gold twisted rope which had been used to seal off an area around the high-ceilinged room. I also noticed a priest far off in the distance seated by a table. Thinking nothing of it, so consumed was I by my desire for holy water, I lifted the rope and ran towards the priest, thinking he would be able to help me on my quest.

The priest was dressed in the traditional long black robes with a skullcap that barely seemed to balance on the crown of his head as he stood up from the table, shouting in Italian at the three of us (Edge and Aisling had followed me under the rope). The priest was startled and, by the expression on his face, horrified that we had entered the sealed-off room. He hastened himself in our direction, still shouting in his language, while firmly clutching a hand to his head in an attempt to hold his little skullcap in place. He placed himself directly in front of us, throwing his arms about the air as if he was having a fit. Edge looked at me and asked what was going on. By this time the priest was ushering the three of us back towards his table, pushing us down into the surrounding seats.

Edge, Aisling and I had become very confused about what was happening. Panicking and trying hard to escape, we stood up to leave but this sent the priest ballistic. He now started to fidget about in his chair, once again swinging his arms about, frowning as he made a shushing noise from his mouth, while screwing up his face and placing a finger to his lips indicating us to silence. At the same time, he beckoned his free hand in a downward motion to advise us that we had to stay seated.

The priest's belligerence was a little unnerving, although we were very shortly to be distracted as the room began to fill with smoke, along with the warm pungent smell of incense floating about in the air. Within seconds a deep melodic chanting had also begun, growing louder and more mystical by the minute. We had stumbled in on a most extraordinary ceremony.

Even now I'm not sure exactly what Edge, Aisling and I witnessed in the Vatican that day in May, but it lasted for more than an hour, and we weren't allowed to move or utter a single sound. We saw holy men dressed in the finest of clothes, each garment rich in textured brocades and colours. Golds, whites, reds and purple robes swept along the ground as the procession led towards the centre of the room. There a diagram had been drawn out across the white marbled floor stones, not unlike ones associated with the occult. Thick black diagonal lines crossed over the middle of the room joining with other thick black markings and symbols. These strange black cryptic-looking images seemed to be placed precisely inside the triangles. As the priests neared the floor markings they began to circle around them.

Each of the high priests wore a different-shaped hat. Some were large and pointed, almost cone shaped; others were wide of brim. The hats obviously denoted their rank within the Church, although they were all ornately trimmed with gold and purple stitching.

The 40 or more elderly men then followed one another around the floor markings in a circular procession, while chanting and swinging the gold-chained chalice, which was still releasing sweet smells of frankincense into the room. Another cardinal (I think) held a gold-coloured rod high in the air. Eventually the parading stopped but the chanting continued, with one of the holy men now going down on all fours, kissing the ground beneath him as he lay down his body spread-eagled out across the diagram in a slightly sinister manner. He was lying there with the other men circling and chanting over him, all the time spilling more of the incense into the air.

As the ceremony came to a close, with all the priests now standing, the chanting became softer until it stopped abruptly, leaving a deadly hush for a moment. Then the holy men all began rushing towards the table and the priest, yelling and screaming among themselves as they looked across at the three of us, obviously wanting to know what we were doing there.

We were eventually evicted from the Vatican, with the skullcapped priest unceremoniously frogmarching us out of the domed room. We were teary-eyed with emotion, hardly able to believe what we had witnessed.

As we climbed into the waiting car, the atmosphere was strained, with Bono and Larry flaming mad, demanding to know what had happened to make me so late, and Dennis almost having a coronary wondering what he was going to tell Ellen, who was waiting back at the hotel, holding the fort with the press and photographers.

Edge calmed them all down, apologising and explaining that we were held captive, going on to recount our amazing story – still finding it hard to believe and comprehend himself. The rest of the party listened attentively.

They were astonished. Bono and Larry both said that they couldn't believe they'd missed out on such an event. They wished that they had seen it for themselves. Bono added, half-jokingly, that he would be back one day to meet the Pope, and would then ask him in person what had taken place. I wonder if he ever did.

Meanwhile, Dennis placed the entire blame for the boys' lateness on me when he explained the incident to Ellen, who was back at the hotel holding the fort, having to appease the press and photographers.

And, for the first time on that tour, I had been accused of something I had actually done. Graciously, I held up my hands.

Chapter 15

A Night in Bono's Bedroom

In every job things soon take on a routine. U2 were flying from Italy on to London where, instead of playing to the 80,000 fans, as seen at the Wembley Stadium, they were now going to perform for just 9,000 fans inside the Wembley Arena.

Talk within the organisation revolved around fixing new dates in order to make the *Joshua Tree* tour more viable, so Paul McGuiness arranged for the band to head straight back to the Americas after ending the Europe tour, money being the dominant factor. The mood of the four band members once they realised that the tour was to be extended was one of despondency. They had thought that the *Joshua Tree* tour would be complete after their Cork gig in August 1987.

Bono, Larry, Edge and Adam had all complained of being tired and stressed out, and their personal lives were also under intense pressure. Backstage in the dressing rooms, the atmosphere was defiant – and depressing. The boys were constantly bickering with each other over things that I thought were trivial.

Bono accused Larry of trying to steal his identity by using the same aftershave as him. Expressing his annoyance, Bono told Larry that, if he put as much effort into copying how he dressed and styled himself, it would go along way towards improving the image of U2. Larry replied that the aftershave had not yet been made exclusively for Bono, and told him that he should shut his mouth. These squabbles started to become the norm, with Larry challenging Bono at every given moment.

With their spirits so low, it was hard to believe that the band was capable of going up on stage and performing at the level that they did, playing in Gothenburg, London, Paris, and then back home in Ireland.

They were preparing to play in The Kings Hall, Belfast. Conversation was now constantly filled with talk of finance, with McGuiness warning the band that if, they wanted to make big money, the large outdoor stadiums of America were the only way to go. To validate the point, Paul arranged for a meeting to be held backstage at London's Wembley Stadium with U2's accountants and financial advisers, O.J. Kilkenny.

Bono was concerned about the 'how and if' of U2 filling

such vast venues. The rest of the band didn't share his worries. As far as they were concerned, as long as they were able to put hefty pay-cheques into their Abbey National accounts, they were unconcerned. Bono was not in agreement with them, although he added that he too wanted to make money. He clearly did not agree with McGuiness's advice, and was worried about the consequences for his and the band's future if U2 were unable to fill the stadiums. If they got it wrong, he said, there would be no money.

Bono asked me what my thoughts were about the band appearing on large monitors when they played huge stadiums, some of which had the capacity to hold 80,000 people or more. At that time, during the late 1980s, it was a novelty to have the promoters hang the large-screened monitors strategically about the venues, affording clear vision to those punters who had paid exactly the same price for their ticket but ended up far from the stage. But many people in the music industry – including Bono – were anti the big screens. My view was that the screened monitors were the way forward, and I said so.

Bono's mood had become dark. Even though I had witnessed his depressions in the past, I had never seen him quite like this. He had become very quiet and introverted, barely communicating with anyone. As he sat alone in the dressing room not wanting to be disturbed, he would often read or write in his notepads. Other times, after I had prepared him for the night's gig, he would sit alone, silently staring out into the room, like he was meditating or lost to another world.

That was, until the tour manager called into the dressing room informing them of the time, which meant that they were now to prepare themselves to go out on stage. They did this in an almost robotic fashion. They would gather in the centre of the dressing room as if nothing was wrong between them, and begin to pep talk each other, in order to get themselves psyched up for their gig. Their gloomy energy would be left behind in the dressing room. Witnessing U2 up on their podiums generating so much euphoria, it was hard to believe that these guys had barely exchanged a 'hello' during the course of the day.

Bono's behaviour at this time made me feel inept and rather awkward, especially after seeing him puking once again. It was moments before he was due on stage. I had walked into the showers to find him vomiting into the sink. It seemed as though this was becoming a habit. I was not only shocked but concerned, and asked him rather awkwardly if he was ill. He said he was just hungover, although I knew he had been fasting, and had also refrained from drinking alcohol. I knew Bono was feeling uncomfortable about his weight gain. This wasn't helped by the fact he had discovered the trousers he had now taken to wearing, although a size larger than his usual jeans, were also fitting rather too snugly.

I became disturbed. Bono had been determined to diet

until he could fit back into his usual trouser size, and it seemed he was taking things to extremes, by making himself ill. I started to realise exactly what lengths he was prepared to go to in order to lose weight and, knowing how secretive he was about everything, I felt I could not mention my findings to anybody else.

Bono had asked me to encourage and help him in devising a diet and exercise programme, although this was absolutely not my field of expertise. And I had already made the point about him getting his own trainer and nutritionist. He had thought that a trainer was a good idea, but also felt it would not go down well with the other band members, and could create some jealousy.

Bono was like any one of us needing support and guidance. I had by now stopped concerning myself with the bizarreness of the situation and just got on with doing my job, becoming wardrobe mistress extraordinaire, as I coaxed and encouraged him relentlessly in his pursuit for a finer physique.

Day by day, I began to feel more like an S&M mistress as I bullied and nagged at him to work out, even reminding him sometimes during the course of his nights of socialising (turning up like a bad penny) that he should be ready for his workout.

Bono had taken to exercising in the dressing rooms of the venues that we were in. He would train with an almost religious intensity, using the elastic and rubber ropes which I had found for him back in Chicago.

Apparently these weight-resistance ropes were a method of training used by boxers, in order to work out their upper arms and torsos. They also served as an aerobic workout when the ropes were used for skipping. This became a part of Bono's daily routine. Not only did his spirits start to lift but he also began to shed some of his unwanted weight – for a little while.

Belfast, 24 May 1987. Emotions were running high, as U2 had flown in from Switzerland to play the first of their gigs in Ireland. It seemed that the whole of Dublin had come up north to see them.

The Hotel Europa was where U2 and their entourage had been booked in to stay, despite its reputation for being the most blown-up hotel in the world. I was not sure if this was why barbed wire surrounded the entire hotel – along with armed guards standing in security boxes which had been erected close to the entrance of the hotel foyer – but nonetheless I was feeling alarmed, bordering on fearful, especially as body frisking was required and carried out each time one entered and left the hotel.

None of these things seemed to deter many other folk, however. The hotel was fully booked, and a lot of the band's guests and family were unable to secure rooms for love or money. The hotel management jokingly remarked that they had taken to renting out their broom cupboards as extra rooms.

Security at the small venue where U2 were playing was unyielding. This created a tense atmosphere. The Kings Hall arena, although only capable of holding 6,000 people, had maintained maximum security, with no detail too trivial to be overlooked. Vigilance was at its height. U2 playing in Northern Ireland at that time required extra caution, to the extent that the Army brought in sniffer dogs before and during the gig.

But the only explosions coming from the Kings Hall that night were from Bono and the band's performance on stage. The atmosphere inside the arena turned from one of nervous tension into an electrifying kind of energy. It was like dynamite seeing family, friends and punters rocking in the aisles as Bono's mellifluous tones belted around the venue, pumping every individual's adrenalin towards fever pitch.

Everybody including myself was caught up in the explosive energy generating out from the gig that night, with Bono, Larry, Edge and Adam seeming to put all of their differences behind them.

The hotel, it soon emerged once we got back, had become overrun with people noisily celebrating Ireland's biggest and most successful export. Folk were spilling out from the hotel bars, jamming the reception area with a party that had apparently started hours earlier with a lot of the band members' family and friends who had been unable to obtain tickets to the gig. And they were all getting well and truly plastered.

I had gone straight up to my room in order to wind up my nightly chores as well as shower and dress myself in some finery befitting the occasion. Alone in the room, I started to become a little spooked, especially as I knew the hotel was constantly being targeted by the IRA and, realising that I did not want to spend the night by myself, unwillingly, I rang one of the girls working from Principal Management's office hoping that she would kindly let me share her room.

Having finalised my sleeping arrangements, I headed, refreshed, out of my room towards the hotel elevators, ready to go down and join in with the celebrations. Suddenly, out of the opened lift tumbled two very drunk men, one of them a close friend of Edge.

Piers was falling about all over the place and only capable of standing with the help of his fellow inebriate, who had somehow managed to keep them both from falling by clutching hold of Piers's shirtsleeve tightly. They rocked and swayed in different directions in an attempt to walk. Miraculously the shirt did not tear as the two of them tried to keep themselves standing upright, unsure where they were heading.

Piers recognised me, which was a miracle in itself as he was so drunk. Incoherently, he informed me that he had been unable to secure lodgings for himself and asked if I could help find him and his friend somewhere to sleep. Thinking nothing of it, I searched inside my handbag for my room key, and handed it over to him, telling him that they could sleep in my room as I was spending the night elsewhere. 'Here,' I said, handing over the key with the room number clearly marked on the key-ring.

'God bless you. God bless you,' were the last words I heard from Piers that night, as I hurried on to the party feeling good that I was able to help him out.

There was only one small problem. I was in possession of duplicate room keys for Bono, Larry Edge and Adam's suites.

After spending almost the entire night partying, the U2 entourage finally retired, worse for wear. Having no gig the following night had allowed most of the entourage to take advantage of a day in bed. But not me. I had a breakfast meeting arranged at 9am in the morning on the insistence of Bono, who was keen to talk about the idea of having a video machine specially built, so that all of their gigs throughout Europe could be videoed. This would allow Bono and I to study U2's performance on stage.

I knocked loudly at Bono's door, not really expecting him to answer it or even be awake. So I was a little startled when it opened almost immediately, with Bono's head staring out from behind a tiny slit of an opening in the door.

Looking even more startled than me, he anxiously beckoned me inside, opening the door wider to let me in, as he took a quick peep out into the hotel corridor, then quickly closed the door behind him.

I asked him if he would like to rearrange the meeting for some other time, politely excusing myself, feeling uncomfortable and desperate to leave the room. Bono's behaviour was very odd. He had a strange look on his face as he insisted that I stay and eat breakfast with him. By this time I wanted to know why he was acting so bizarrely. He told me to order some food and coffee from room service, as he was feeling completely freaked out. He kept apologising, over and over, and continued pacing the room as he told me that he'd had a nasty experience during the night.

He told me that he thought some men had broken into his room. He was certain, he said, that there were men talking and wandering around his bed. He mentioned how his duvet cover had been lifted off him, making him feel totally vulnerable. He said he had been too afraid to open his eyes but heard the men repeat his name several times. Apparently the men were also throwing pieces of furniture around, and had smashed up a table lamp in the ruckus. At least that's what he thought. Because, he explained, he was so pissed he was not sure if it had really happened or if he'd had a nightmare.

'Lola, I have to stop the drinking,' he said, acting really sorry for himself, obviously upset that he did not know if something had occurred in his room.

'Look,' I said, pointing excitedly to the broken lamp lying smashed on the floor. 'You were not dreaming. Somebody was in here. But who could it have been?' I was hoping this would make him feel better, but by this stage I was doing nothing to calm him or the situation down.

In fact, we were both getting more and more paranoid. Bono started to wonder if the IRA had attempted to kidnap him and, as we sat and munched away at our breakfast, we started pondering the awful threat of an IRA kidnap, and Bono fretted about the publicity that the news would cause.

I couldn't have been more mortified if I had seen demons, when Bono mentioned that one of the voices sounded very much like Piers.

The repercussions of my good deed were about to come back and haunt me. I immediately downed my cutlery, chomping away at the last piece of toast in my mouth, trying hard not to choke as I gulped it down. I cupped both hands over my mouth as I gasped with the sudden shock of the situation.

Now it was I who was apologising, as well as laughing with nervous energy. I felt like a complete fool, embarrassed, as I had to sit there and explain to Bono the previous night's meeting with Piers. I told Bono how I had given Piers the key to my room but had obviously fucked up and mistakenly handed over Bono's room key instead.

What a schmuck I was.

Thankfully, by this time, Bono was in fits of laughter, relieved at the outcome. He said that he had heard of dumb blondes, but that he had one dumb brunette working for him, handing his room key over to some drunken Irish bastards. 'Most rock stars have pretty women running around their bedrooms at night, Lola,' he said, laughing even harder, barely able to believe the farce that had taken place in his room that night.

Bono's thoughts now drifted back to the lack of security around him, and he had said, 'So much for security.'

Once again he became amused or hysterical as he clutched his sides with laughter. I suspect he was relieved that it was not a part of some elaborate IRA kidnap plot.

We never got around to discussing any business that morning, but as I was leaving his suite Bono looked at me inquisitively and asked if something was going on between Piers and me. More laughter. It was turning into a farce.

It was many gigs and some moons later before I bumped into Piers again, who immediately rushed up to ask me, 'What the hell was Bono doing in my bed that night?' With a big smile on his face he began to tell me what had gone down that night in the Hotel Europa. I told him I had heard about it, recapping to him Bono's take on it all. We both stood there roaring with laughter. How could a good deed have gone so wrong?

Piers began to give his side of the story. He and his friend managed to make their way to the room number on the key. On entering the room, they fumbled and stumbled about in the dark searching for the light switch, and accidentally knocked the furniture about in their search. Piers, suddenly in urgent need of the loo, remembered that as he had entered the suite he had seen the bathroom and headed straight for it, leaving his mate to continue his stumbling. Eventually the friend found a lamp on top of a table and, in the process of attempting to switch it on, smashed it. By this time Piers was in the middle of the room and, on discovering the light switch, had turned it on, to find a body in the bed. Perplexed about why somebody else was in the bed that they had thought was meant for them, they went over to have a closer inspection. On lifting the covers and discovering Bono naked and asleep, they were shocked and confused and apparently just stood there, over the bed, repeating Bono's name to each other: 'Bejesus. It's Bono.' 'Bejesus. It's Bono.' After this, they turned to flee but, in their desperate attempt, smashed into more furniture, sending objects flying across the room. More noisy, Piers said, they could not have been.

'So, Lola,' Piers enquired after finishing his story, 'you still haven't answered my question. What was Bono doing in your bed?'

Chapter 16

I'm a Celebrity Stylist,
Get Me Out of Here

U2 rocked their way across Europe doing no wrong. There were plaudits wherever they went. It seemed that Bono ruled the world and everybody associated with him and U2 were caught up in the euphoria.

I thanked my sensible working-class background for allowing me to hold on to the fact that Bono, Edge, Larry and Adam were my employers. I did not make the mistake of assuming they were my best friends.

Even though a lot of us were trying not to live our lives in the reflected glory of it all, it was extremely difficult. The very mention of Bono's name opened doors, and nothing, it seemed, was impossible. To keep one's feet on the ground was harder for some of the entourage than others. Sometimes some of their more mundane yet behind-the-scenes tasks broke down to the point of becoming farcical.

How Bono and the boys ended up on stage performing some nights amazed me, especially after witnessing, and sometimes even causing, the disasters that occurred throughout the course the day.

A prime example of this occurred during an attempted departure from Madrid. The entire U2 entourage had left the Palace Hotel in Madrid a day ahead of Finton and me. With a few days off before their gig in the South of France, they were headed for the hills of Montpelier. Bono and the boys were looking to relax in the most sumptuous of hotels. In fact, it was a castle, situated on the hills of Vieux Castellion. It had the most splendid views across and beyond the pastures of Montpelier. Looking out to the south, you could still see the remains of an ancient aqueduct, which had long been used to bring the water down from the mountains in order to serve the rest of the southern region. The castle had only ten – candlelit – bedrooms to accommodate their guests, and a chef whose reputation was unsurpassed.

I felt very privileged when I was informed that I was to stay there as well. So I hastily tried to wind up my work in Madrid and hurry on to the south of France. With Finton's help, I didn't anticipate there being any problems.

As our flight was not until the early evening, Finton and I used the day to relax. We were *lean*, as we strolled around Madrid without a care in the world, before checking out the art and sculpture that was on show in Madrid's famous Prado Museum, and then stopping to dine al fresco in the warm summer sun. We finished off with some retail therapy. It had been a splendid afternoon – unlike the start of the morning, when I had encountered the first of the problems that were to raise their ugly heads that day.

As we were preparing to leave the hotel for our stroll, Finton and me were informed by the hotel management that checkout time was at noon, and that there would be no available space to store our belongings. With over 20 pieces of luggage to our names, we had some belongings. (It was surprising how quickly, once U2 had departed from the hotel, that things got back to normal. The star treatment was over.) It took a great deal of negotiation to get them to store the luggage. You'd have thought this would be routine for a hotel of such calibre, but they didn't want anything to do with so many cases, unless, of course, I paid for a room for an extra day. My allowance didn't grant me such privileges. A little bit of flamingo-style foot-stamping had to take place and did the trick.

Eventually, after our beautiful July day spent looking around Madrid, Finton and I headed back early to the hotel so we would be ahead of time for the transport that Theresa was supposed to have arranged for us. But we could not get near the hotel. There was a bomb scare – Basque terrorists, apparently – and the hotel had been evacuated. Alarmed, and wondering what we should do (and in the days before mobiles), I headed for the public phones to call the transport company. I was told that no vehicles had been arranged for us, and that they would not have enough cars available to ferry Finton, me or even the luggage.

I tried to stay calm and sort out how we would be able to get the 16 pieces of luggage (not including mine and Finton's suitcases), as well as ourselves, out of Madrid. Most normal-thinking people would have been considering taxis by this stage, but when you've been on the road for a while, with your transport always arranged, you begin to get a bit retarded – well, I did.

Finton and I were standing well back from the huge crowd that had now gathered outside the hotel – I had better plans for my death, being blown up trying to rescue Bono's clothes was certainly not among them.

Having so much gear to clear through customs was going to prove a nightmare, and would mean that we would need to be at the airport a lot earlier than our 7pm flight. I began to panic.

Time was running out. It was 4pm, and the hotel had just been given the all-clear. Finton and I ran around the streets close to the hotel trying to flag down taxis. With the concierge's help, we eventually managed to pile the luggage into six cabs. We decided we would accompany some of the luggage, but would each take separate taxis. I didn't want to take any risks with most of U2's stage wardrobe and, what with the morning's events having already fucked everything up, I began to have an ominous feeling about the rest of the day.

Letting the luggage out of my sight did not sit entirely comfortably with me, and with very little Spanish under my belt I had asked the hotel concierge not only to advise each of the drivers of our destination but also to explain the predicament we were in.

Our taxi convoy headed off, so I thought, to Madrid's International Airport. My last words to Finton were to keep an eye on the suitcases.

Arriving at Madrid International Airport, I discovered two things: first, the other cars had not yet arrived; and, second the luggage handlers and airport staff were on strike, which meant that the luggage trolleys were out of service. This proved to be a huge problem and all my pleading and financial encouragement to the taxi drivers to stay and help was refused.

But I didn't think that I had too much to worry about just yet. I felt certain that Finton would show up very shortly.

The clock ticked away the minutes. Eventually I knew our flight out of Madrid was lost.

I had been pacing the pavement for more than an hour and a half. Keeping a teary eye on our load of trunks and luggage bags, which the taxi driver had stacked near to the main entrance of the airport, I began to fear for Finton's life, believing him to have been fatally injured in a car accident. It was the only possible explanation for the delay of almost two hours. I was beside myself.

I eventually decided to risk leaving the luggage unattended and try placing a call through to the south of France, hoping I would be able to get hold of the tour manger whose instructions, under such dire circumstances, I wanted to take.

Frantically searching for a public phone, I spotted trunks and luggage stacked unusually high. Case upon case had been piled up, creating the effect of a wall. The barrier of bags looked strangely familiar – and they seemed to be slowly shuffling themselves in my direction. I went over to take a closer look.

I had found Finton. Alive! He was behind the wall of luggage, leaning himself against the bags as he gently pushed and manoeuvred the heavy load forward. Since he couldn't possibly lift, or move, all of the luggage, or even keep everything together, he had devised this, his own method.

I didn't know whether to hit him, kiss him or just stand there relieved that he was alive. I think I did all three.

Finton had a horrified look upon his face, as he explained to me that the driver had asked him which airport he wanted. Uncertain where Montpelier was, he had told the driver to take him to Madrid's internal flights airport, which was a long way off from the International Airport where we were meant to be.

'Finton,' I exclaimed, 'where the fuck is Montpelier?'

'The south of France,' he replied.

'Well, what was the complication?' I was yelling and

throwing my hands in the air. 'You couldn't possibly believe that France was in Spain – could you?'

I was exasperated and feeling like James Bond's sister. Trying to get us both out of Madrid felt like *The Krypton Factor* – it was one assault course after the other.

With the fear still in his voice, Finton went on to explain that, on realising he had gone to the wrong airport, and also having discovered the airport staff's strike, he had panicked. And not knowing what to do, he began crying, with my words of warning when we had parted from the hotel ('Do not let the bags out of your sight!') still ringing in his ears. So he didn't.

But our nightmare did not stop there. We were to spend another five hours at Madrid International Airport, as I attempted to purchase some new tickets for both of us, and clear our luggage through customs. The vast quantity of bags and trunks had caused complications for the skeletal staff that were left manning the airport.

The flight that we eventually got booked on took off, then aborted halfway up in the air. The aircraft landed with a thump as the body of the plane careered down on to the tarmac and then, without any prior warning, took off again. By this time I was in desperate need of Prozac or a drink – but definitely *something*. My nerves were shot to pieces as we finally landed safely – minus all our luggage – in the south of France. I was done for.

Theresa had arranged for a fleet of luxury cars with uniformed chauffeurs to meet us at the airport, ready to collect and drive both of us, along with our luggage, up to the hills of Castellion and the castle. Only our luggage was lost. Not one of our bags had arrived.

Strangling Theresa sprang to mind.

As we both finally entered the castle's courtyard in the early hours of the morning, dishevelled and tired, we were playfully grabbed by the U2 security men, who proceeded to lift us both high in the air. With everyone else clapping and cheering as they welcomed us home, we were ceremoniously thrown fully clothed into the cold pool water. Cheers and cries from Bono and the band to let the party commence echoed across the range.

I shuddered in the cool night air, feeling like some kind of hero.

All this just to get a band dressed for a gig, I laughed to myself.

Chapter 17

Back in the USA

I had never witnessed such madness in my life. U2 were back in the United States to play at the massive outdoor stadiums McGuiness had so desperately wanted. And it was a great success. Bono, Larry, Edge and Adam were unable to walk the streets or go into a restaurant to eat without being mobbed by screaming fans. They had all become huge stars. And the boys were loving the adulation.

Every hotel that we stayed in had to have the entrance roped off and security tightened, with the police often called in to control the hundreds of fans that had taken to camping outside the hotels. Some would spend the entire night, even chanting Bono's name in the hope that they would be able to catch a glimpse of him. Some of the more affluent punters would book into the hotel in the hope of fulfilling their dreams and meeting Bono face to face.

Diehard devotees of the band had ways of sourcing information about their idols' activities by means that only they knew. They were even able to find out the individual names of the U2 crew members. And anyone who was associated with the band would get hassled as the fans pleaded and cried to you, at times throwing themselves at your feet for Bono's autograph. It could get quite scary. It was amazing to me the lengths a devoted follower would go to.

But meanwhile, things back on the ranch were not so cosy. An all-out war was raging inside the U2 organisation, with internal bickering between U2's American office staff, headed by Ellen Darst, and the Dublin-based management. U2 had become huge in the States, beyond even Bono's wildest dream, and the office staff, whose responsibility was obviously to keep the tour afloat and rolling, were now divided into two camps: USA versus Ireland. And, if things didn't get done quite as professionally as they should have before the squabbles, they now began to get even worse. You did not know who to go to, in order to accomplish any particular task. If something needed fixing it would never get done and, if you challenged any of the girls about it, they would just smile sweetly and apologise, pretending that they had accidentally overlooked your request, all the time knowing that they had the power to do exactly as they pleased. If it caused a fuck-up for the band then so be it. Their arguments affected us all in one way or another.

Now, for me to acquire a U2 ticket and backstage pass for a gig – normally a routine request by me to Ellen's office, and also one of my entitlements – had became quite a trial. Using tickets – a widely used method of payment inside the music industry – as a kind of bribe had always helped me attain unreasonable demands, especially when I needed a tailor in New York to help me out, when Bono had been asked to attend a function at very late notice. Bono's suit no longer fitted him, it was too small, so there was some urgency in getting a replacement made up. The tailor had agreed, after a single fitting, to help make another, doing whatever was needed to have the suit ready for the following night. Like a true professional he kept his word, delivering the exquisitely tailored suit by the time agreed.

It was with great embarrassment that I learned, some months later when I approached the tailor to carry out some more work, that he had not been able to attend the gig, as there were no tickets left for him or his wife as I had promised.

The explanation offered by Ellen's office staff was that it was an oversight.

The arguments seemed petty but the fight for power was mighty, and if I had kept a low profile in the past I was going to keep an even lower one now. I tried to keep my nose clean and went about my business. After all, being back in the States was a lot of fun and I wanted to enjoy it.

Bono's moods and weight gain continued swinging like a clock's pendulum, and so too did my shopping trips, as I was constantly on the lookout for new clothes that would accommodate the lead singer of U2's fluctuating bodyweight.

My shopping expeditions had to be very low key because, if one of the sales assistants got wind of who I was buying the clothes for, within seconds there were TV news crews and newspaper reporters all over the store, causing pandemonium. This I had the misfortune to experience.

It was in Los Angeles and I was in the Beverly Hills complex, shopping for some very basic supplies, like toiletries and aftershaves, when a U2 crew member spotted me at the perfumery counter. Having exchanged very quick hellos, we mentioned something very general that gave the sales assistant some clue as to who I was shopping for. This information was obviously passed on to her boss, who must have thought, like a true capitalist, what splendid publicity it would be for the store to be mentioned in connection with U2. And they must have informed the local TV station who turned up just seconds after I had left the store. In the meantime I was making my way back to the car, when I heard somebody call my name (the sales assistant must have got the information from my credit card). A young woman was running towards me. She was obviously from a TV crew, as she was being followed by her colleagues who were holding lighting equipment and other paraphernalia with the TV station's logo blazed across it. I had now started to run, feeling like an escaped convict and racing off in no particular direction, trying hard to remember where the chauffeur had parked the car. This information eluding me, I nervously managed to jump into the back seat of somebody else's car as they were attempting to leave the shopping centre's parking lot.

The shocked look on the face of my unsuspecting accomplice was classic, but I soon calmed her down, when I pointed to the news crew, who were running towards us, and explained my situation. Now believing that I was not some lunatic, they helped me escape, and in return I promised her some U2 tickets.

In the event I found, not for the first time, that tickets were not available for me to keep my promise.

Chapter 18

A Night to Remember

Despite the glare of publicity and all the internal politics of the U2 organisation, and although Bono and the band had been booked to play in the larger outdoor stadiums of America, the occasional smaller gig reminded me what it was all about.

The best of these was played inside the belly of the McNichols Arena in Denver, Colorado, in front of 10,000 screaming fans and the film crew who were producing live footage of U2's gigs.

After witnessing Bono, Edge, Larry and Adam's performance on stage that night, it was easy to see why U2 had been named the world's best live rock band.

The intensity of Robert Brinkmann's strategically thought-out, black and white lighting enhancing the silhouetted figures of Bono, Edge and Adam, whilst beaming pure white rays of light down on to the face, hands and drum kit of Larry Mullin Jnr did not go unnoticed. Nor did the dramatics of Edge, ripping and curling through the chords of his electric guitar as if every chord he plucked sent an electric current through his body, sending him contorting and twisting about the stage like a whirling dervish. This was only to be calmed by the perfectly timed interruption of Adam's bass. The deep, melodic tones resonating from this deftly played instrument assisted in soothing and complementing the electric shrill.

Bono, meanwhile, worked the rest of the stage. Running about to the soaring cacophony, he jumped from east to west, leaping from the different-levelled podiums that were spotted about the stage, resembling a deranged animal.

He appeared to be trying to escape the beating rhythms of his own band as he ran randomly about the arena belting out the lyrics from 'The Hands of Love', as perspiration seeped from every pore in his body. The unique, mellifluous voice paused only for an intake of breath when he almost slipped on one of the pools of his own sweat that had formed, like puddles, indiscriminately about the stage.

Finally, like a man possessed, Bono suddenly and quite unexpectedly stopped and stood still for a second, throwing back his head violently, sending limp wet strands of hair off his face. Then, without any warning, he strutted almost belligerently across to the centre of the stage, tearing the soaking wet tee shirt he was wearing from his body, before discarding it on the ground like a rag. Equipped now with only his Gibson hung over his naked shoulder, he broke into a mindblowing rendition of 'Gloria'.

Once again he belted out the words, almost sending them to kingdom come, so as to be heard above the thunderous roars and foot stomping reverberating from the 10,000 hysterical fans.

That night Bono, along with Edge, Larry and Adam, contorted their bodies and instruments about the stage almost as if they were possessed by some higher being. For anyone there, it was a night to remember. As I witnessed my employers at work, my eyes misted over, and a few proud tears fell.

What made one gig different from any other was hard to say, and was the topic of many discussions between band and crew. They would analyse for days on end, going over the acoustics of a venue, the size and participation of the crowd, even examining the set list in order to try and understand what elusive magic had created such a magnificent night's performance. No stone would be left unturned in the quest to find out why one night's gig blew other nights away. I always thought Bono's gut instinct for being able to read his audience and then feed them back what they had come to hear played a major part in the equation. But no definitive practical reasons were ever found.

Bono was quite superstitious, and his own theory was that if a gig had gone exceptionally well he would stick to the winning format and replicate the exact same set list at the very next venue. This didn't always go down well with their sound engineer, Joe.

Joe would often point out to Bono, as they were rehearsing at the afternoon soundchecks, what songs he felt the particular venue could carry. Sometimes he even advised Bono to forgo the more iconic of the U2 numbers because he felt the unique sound so associated with these songs would not be able to be duplicated at the location due to its acoustics.

Bono would sometimes heed the advice of his much-respected crew member. Other times his burning desire to go with what he felt the audience would love, regardless of the sound quality, took precedence. He felt a certain obligation to his fans, and came to the conclusion that they were never fully satisfied unless numbers like 'With or Without You' or 'I Still Haven't Found What I'm looking For' were included.

The set list was a much-debated topic among the band, especially as Bono would sometimes change the entire set on a whim, advising his crew and stagehands of his change of heart at dangerously short notice. This he would usually put down to a gut feeling he had about the venue they were in, either that or he would say that his throat was playing up and his voice just wouldn't be able to handle a specific set of songs.

And so the set list would be arranged accordingly.

Sometimes this would involve iconic numbers being taken out of the set as a deliberate ploy to whip the already excited crowd into a frenzy. The idea was that, when the band reappeared for an encore, Bono would be the last to walk back on stage, walking slowly so as to allow his entire body to be silhouetted by the dramatic, harsh, halogen lights. This image, accompanied by a long intro into 'With or Without You', which the punters had feared they weren't going to hear, created such an explosion of emotion that it almost brought down the house.

Pandemonium broke out inside the Denver arena, sending the levels of noise right off the Richter scale, and almost certainly seeing damage inflicted on an eardrum or two.

Over the years, I have been privy to many a brilliant gig, but never have I quite witnessed anything that compared to that evening. I felt that there was almost certainly a higher presence in attendance that night.

Chapter 19

Drama Off Stage

Whilst things behind the scenes of the U2 organisation were smouldering but looking like they were about to ignite, Bono, Larry, Edge and Adam were caught in their own fire. The band's popularity was at an all-time high. It had come to the point in their career where it seemed they could do no wrong. But there was a price to pay. Their every action came under intense public scrutiny. And this made them all paranoid, to the extent that they could not give an interview, have a photo taken or even step outside of their hotel rooms without seeking each other's – or a team of advisers' – approval. Whereas back in Europe the band hardly socialised with each other, they had now turned in the opposite direction, seeking Bono's guidance at every turn, be it on the way they looked, the way they spoke or what to say about themselves in print.

Bono's torment within himself was crippling him. Outwardly, he tried to project to the world that he didn't give a damn about what anybody else thought of him or U2, giving the impression that they were a 'take it or leave'-type of band. But deep down he cared, and he cared deeply. He was concerned about what the ordinary person on the street thought and said about him. Bono had even asked me what my own friends' views were on him, soliciting me for an honest answer.

He had reached the stage where accepting a music award became debatable, seeking advice from the don of Trinity University back in Ireland on whether to accept an award that U2 had been nominated for, on the basis that it was English. Bono needed and wanted to be schooled in articulating political rhetoric. He was desperate to portray to the world that he was acting politically correctly. This was the cause of a lot of conflict between him and the other band members. Basically the boys were gnawing over every aspect of U2's image to the point of obsession.

With Bono struggling with his weight and Ellen with her muscle, things were soon to climax when some daily tabloids displayed some rather unflattering pictures of Bono and the band. The ludicrous-looking pictures had made Bono emerge looking fat and clown-like, because they had been shot from an angle that had given the viewer the impression that the tip of the microphone was attached to his nose. To make matter worse, Larry was in the same photograph looking like his ears belonged to Dumbo the elephant, because some props that had been situated behind his drum kit had also been included in his headshot.

With the band's paranoia at an all-time high, Bono was not amused. He went ballistic, screaming and shouting at Ellen, demanding to know if she had cataracts in her eyes, and not understanding how she could possibly have approved the pictures.

It was the responsibility of Ellen's office to deal with all the band's publicity. This included hand-picking the photographers who were allowed to take the band's pictures. In return, U2's management maintained ownership of all the film, along with quality control on all the photos and images that were taken and eventually distributed on for circulation.

Bono called a meeting (this was becoming a very normal occurrence as Bono grew more concerned about things with each passing day). He wanted McGuiness, Ellen and me to attend.

What transpired at the meeting was that Bono informed Ellen that I was to take control of U2's entire aesthetic image. This meant that I was now to have the additional task of sorting and approving every single U2 photograph. This was a daunting prospect and the first I'd heard about it. With communication between Ellen and me leaving a lot to be desired, I was not happy at the thought of having any dealings with her, let alone her having to seek my authorisation on band photographs. I would be in need of a minder, for now it was Ellen who was not amused.

This had all taken place earlier in the day back in Chicago's Four Seasons Hotel, but nonetheless it was 3am in the wee hours of the morning when there was a knock at my door. I thought I was hallucinating when I opened it to see Ellen standing before me. She was holding a heavy-looking film projector in her arms, and was accompanied by a bellboy, who was himself controlling a trolley full of cardboard boxes. These, I was very soon to learn, held thousands of film slides and transparencies of Bono and U2.

'Here,' she said, pushing the projector towards me. 'These are your responsibility now.' And she ushered and directed the bellhop to dump the several loads of boxes into my room. 'Oh by the way,' she added, 'I will be needing your approval on six shots of Bono and the band by tomorrow afternoon. So when you've worked your way through looking at that lot, do let me have your selection. You do know how to use a projector, don't you?'

Not waiting for my reply, Ellen walked off, turning around only to wish me goodnight.

Completely overwhelmed, I began to cry. The tears came without any warning. I put my silly reaction down to the early hour, as well as the overwhelming sight of boxes that were now stacked about the room. I was completely exasperated and I wondered how I could possibly meet her demands as well as execute my own tasks.

During this time I was also in possession of a rather large flight case, containing the custom-built video player, which Bono had insisted travelled everywhere with me. This allowed me arbitrary viewing of the nightly taped U2 gigs. Distressed, my crying had now grown into full sobs, when suddenly I decided to go into battle mode. I dried my weeping eyes, disregarding the fact that it was 4am in the morning and that I was dressed in PJs, marched along to her room, assisted coincidentally by the same bellboy that had earlier helped her.

I delivered back into Ellen's possession the projector along with the boxes of film.

It was absolutely classic seeing her, weary-eyed from sleep, hunched over as she answered the door, dazed and confused, wondering what was going on. Ignoring her, I directed the bellboy into her room to dispose of my burden. Then in my haughtiest tone, I declared that she could select her own choice of photos and when I had a moment I would take a look at them. With that, I strode off bidding her a good morning.

'Oh Ellen,' I added.

'Yes,' she croaked.

'I don't know how to use a projector.'

The tabloid photographs had left a bad taste in Bono's mouth. With him becoming more intense and serious, and constantly concerned with his appearance, he had instructed a member of his crew to start religiously videoing every single gig. Bono had become doubtful about his and the band's stage performance, to the point where he felt he needed to document their entire set.

This video was for my benefit. I was to study the contents, focusing in on Bono, and then report back to him, in our daily meeting, any findings that would help perfect his performance and appearance. But I had no masterplan that could increase Bono's height and make him appear 6ft tall, with a lean, toned skeleton. Because basically this was what it all came down to.

Chapter 20

Fame and its Foibles

What Bono lacked in stature, barely measuring in at 5ft 7in, he certainly made up for in personality. But this was never enough for the man who was to be voted the No. 1 most powerful man in his industry, as well as being nominated for the Nobel Peace Prize.

Bono was incredibly concerned about his look and image, which at times left him deeply depressed. These insecurities drove him to obsessiveness: one day it would be that his hair wasn't right; the following day he would be beside himself about his weight. This powerful, talented man had always suffered from low self-esteem, but now it was intensified because he had film crews and cameras in his face, filming the *Rattle and Hum* movie. Sometimes, after a gig, instead of attending the after-show party, Bono would go back to his hotel room and sit quietly alone, not wanting to face people.

After the incident with the awful tabloid pictures, Bono instructed me to be vigilant, especially when the film crew or cameras were around him. He told me to step in and take charge, so as to place him in a position where he would appear taller. Bono also wanted me to create an image for the band that would stand the test of time.

Needing constant reassurance from me about how he looked and performed on stage, Bono required me to be on hand at all times. This caused even more insecurity with Ellen and her management, and would have consequences for me further into the tour.

There were times that I found it bizarre, me sitting alone with this idol who was worshipped and adored by millions, listening to him talk about his life and loves. Sometimes we would talk for hours. It would not always be about work, but about topics such as his dreams, which at times were erotic fantasies – almost always centred on Madonna, with whom he had become besotted. Bono's anxiety peaked.

During our meetings, Bono continued to ask me to source information on plastic surgeons. His vanity was still getting the better of him, especially after his accident in Arizona, where he had fallen on stage cracking his chin open, which had required stitches.

Bono's concern with his height was to manifest itself whilst we were backstage in New Jersey. Moments before the band were due on stage, Bono was informed of the celebrity guests attending that night's gig. This was usual practice for the U2 press office, which told him that Bruce Springsteen was in the audience and wanted to be introduced to him. On being told this, Bono began to pace the side of the stage, and then motioned me over. He was extremely agitated. Halting for a moment, he asked me what I could do about it. 'About what?' I enquired, perplexed, and panicking slightly because I couldn't grasp his problem. Bono resumed striding backwards and forwards, nervously interlocking his fingers together. Then he turned and said to me earnestly that he had to be taller than Bruce Springsteen.

Hmmm. A strange request, I thought, as I was his stylist, not David Blaine the magician. I knew that, though I could joke with Bono about many things, it would not be appropriate at that moment to suggest a stretching device. Instead I said, tongue-in-cheek, that the only thing I could propose at such late notice was for him to wear a pair of my high-heel shoes. To my surprise, he thought it a very good idea, and was prepared to jam his feet into my Manolo Blahniks.

Bono's spirits lifted as he stepped on stage with my reassurance that by the time he had completed his set, the shoes would be in my possession. I rapidly arranged for a courier to collect the footwear from the hotel back in New York, and deliver them with haste to Meadowlands where U2 were performing.

That evening I continued with my work routine, laying out the boys' clothes for the after-show party, taking particular care to source a pair of trousers for Bono that had a longer leg length, so that the shoes he would be wearing would not be visible.

On delivery of the bright red heels, Bono attempted to wedge his feet into the delicate footwear in preparation for a practice strut, but with the shoes too narrow for his feet, and the additional gaffer tape that I had bound them on with, he hadn't been able to balance himself at all well. Bono's lack of poise meant that we had to sit and devise a plan which would allow him to pull off the farce without him looking like a drag queen.

The consensus was that, on meeting Bruce Springsteen, Bono would remain seated, standing only to shake his hand.

The shoe plan was to be repeated several times throughout the tour, albeit with a more accommodating heel, until finally I commissioned the late John Moore to hand-make all of Bono's footwear (by this time, my shoes were taking a heavy beating). From now on, his shoes and boots were to be made with raised insoles and wedges that would afford him both height and comfort.

Despite the setbacks, I was enjoying my work. And,

although my relationship with Ellen and Principal Management was not all that I could have wished for, the bond between me and the other band members had evolved. I was now advising as well as clothes shopping for Larry, Edge and Adam.

This was what Bono had wanted from the start. But, as he had not communicated his long-term vision to the group, they just viewed his demands as forcefulness. And being ordered by Bono to have me shop for their clothes did not help matters. Initially it had made Larry, Edge and Adam resentful towards me.

As my relationship with the boys grew, so did my job description. One of my roles developed into being counsellor-cum-confidante, with each of the boys starting to seek my counsel on private matters concerning their lives.

I guess this was not altogether surprising, with me becoming a kind of mother figure for them. This was probably accentuated by the fact I was shopping for their clothes – right down to their smalls, in itself a very personal act – which quickly broke down any inhibitions.

Bono, Larry, Edge and Adam had one thing in common. They all wanted to appear sexy and, at various times, had all hinted that they wanted me to help them achieve this.

We were in Chicago, staying at the Ritz Carlton, when Edge had called round to my room wanting to chat. He was in low spirits, and mentioned that things between him and his wife were not good. Edge was a very sensitive character, and clearly upset by this. It was hard to know what to say to comfort him, especially after he had mentioned how he felt not only vulnerable but under pressure to perform well and look good the entire time. Edge was finding living in the spotlight difficult. He didn't feel like getting up on stage and pretending he was enjoying himself. All he really wanted to do at that time was crawl under a rock and hide.

Going up on stage exacerbated his lack of confidence. This led to him asking me in earnest to help him look sexy. I replied there was nothing I could do to help him in that department. Especially since I had already told him that I believed he was.

Edge believed that his thinning hair was the result of a lot of his personal problems, and felt sure that if he sought professional help with his baldness, it would have an effect on those other areas of his life. With that in mind, he sent me off in search of a trichologist.

I gathered the required information, and Edge's approval, and booked an appointment with a London-based hair specialist. Only when I informed Edge of his appointment did he begin to feel there was a dilemma. He was afraid that the press would get wind of his hair predicament. He was filled with paranoia, having already elicited a promise from me that I wouldn't breathe a word about it to the other band members.

This was not a problem but after I booked and

confirmed Edge's appointment, he insisted that I attend in his place. I was concerned, especially as I had booked the meeting under a male pseudonym and possessed a head full of flowing, healthy locks.

Still, on a cool summer's day in June, I attended the hair specialist's clinic that was situated just off Mayfair in London. I felt rather awkward as I sat in the clinic's waiting room, knowing that the specialist's next client's hair was tucked inside my handbag. Edge had devised a plan whereby I would hand the specialist his cut hair samples, which he had given to me, wrapped up in newspaper.

The normal procedure at the clinic was for the client to sit before the specialist who would then proceed to examine their scalp and hair. This time, the client's hair was placed into the palm of his hand.

The specialist's manner suggested that he felt the person I was representing had lost more than just his hair – especially if the client believed that he would be able to diagnose any type of treatment from the dead hair samples.

All was not lost, however. The doctor explained to me that as he would still be billing for the consultation, I might as well have my own hair analysed.

I had, no objection. In fact, I rather enjoyed the luxury of having lotions and potions made specifically for my hair and scalp. I walked away from the clinic laden with my own specialised treatments.

Adam had difficulty in waking. Often, even though it was late afternoon and he was supposed to be at the venue for the soundcheck, he was still in the hotel – in his bed. This left a lot of people frustrated, not least the U2 tour manager, whose job it was to mummy him into getting up and moving. Adam was also of great concern to Bono. The band members were involved in many discussions about his waywardness.

I had felt sorry for Adam. He was the only member of the band who was without a relationship. Not that a relationship was everything, but he often mentioned that he would like to have a partner – someone with whom he could share his success.

When Adam discovered that I was friends with the singer Sade's brother, he nagged at me to try and arrange a date for him, telling me he really fancied Sade. I didn't have the heart to tell him that Sade didn't fancy him.

I never really felt comfortable around Adam, and I think that was because Adam was never really felt comfortable around himself.

He had the strangest of habits. One of them I discovered by accident. He would always walk around with a threadbare sock. I don't mean that he wore it, although he would occasionally. The mashed-up socks would be carried around with him, usually inside one of his jacket pockets. If he didn't wear a jacket, he would wear the moth-eaten things. But whichever way, the socks went everywhere with him. These socks, although

rom my earliest days I knew that I was not going to sit behind a desk in an office. I
anted freedom. My father (*top right*) was a well-known character in the East End, and
ad links with the Kray twins. I lost my first job because he poured a plate of hot egg
nd chips over my boss's head during a card-game dispute…

Paul Hewson – known to the world as Bono – all dressed up the Lola Cashman way.

Top: Edge on the road.

Bottom left: Larry Mullen Jr – not getting the hump this time, but clutching his tambourine backstage.

Bottom right: Adam Clayton – I'd soon find out that his passion for music was almost outdone by his passion for socks! – with Edge performing in the background.

The scenes that awaited the band as we toured the world.

op: Me aboard U2's personal jet.

ottom: When the band's support group failed to show, U2 decided to support
emselves, with a bit of sartorial help from yours truly.

Left: Out shopping for the band.

Top right: The agonising decisions of being on tour – which Limo shall I take today?

Bottom right: Bono prepares himself for the cameras in San Francisco.

Top left: Just one of U2's many set lists.

Top right: The backstage pass that gave me full access to the band.

Bottom: Larking around with Edge.

After the rigours of touring with the world's biggest band, I had to get away from it all. I did this on a remote cattle farm in Australia, while Bono and U2 continued to amaze audiences around the world. I still haven't found what I'm looking for – but I'm close...

barely hanging together by a thread, were Adam's comfort blanket.

Once, when we had been staying in Manhattan, in a hotel on 52nd Street, Adam approached me, asking me to buy him some new clothes. He also mentioned that he wanted some socks. There was nothing unusual about this. With most of the band's clothes living in their wardrobe flight cases and only becoming available when they had been unloaded at the venue they were playing in, I often had to buy outfits for each of the boys. Especially with them receiving so many unexpected invitations. They only ever carried a few casual clothes around in their holdalls.

So I went shopping. Searching the streets of New York for interesting items of clothes, I found Adam a variety of items, including socks. I made my way to his suite in order to unpack the clothes. On doing so I replaced his old threadbare socks and knickers with the brand new ones. I put the nasty old things into the now emptied shopping bag, which I placed outside his hotel door for the maid to dispose of. I really didn't know at the time how precious they were to him.

The band had a few nights off, and we were all taking advantage of some free time. I arranged to meet friends for an early evening dinner at a new restaurant that had just opened on Canal Street. We were just about to be seated at the table, when the Maitre'd, came over, and informed our party that there was a telephone call for Lola.

It was Adam, and he sounded very upset asking where his old socks were.

Oh no. I felt sick. I made my excuses and left the restaurant. I jumped in a cab and headed back to the hotel.

As soon as I entered the foyer of the Omni Berkshire, I did not make my way to Adam, but instead sought the help of Chris the concierge – who owed me. I had arranged a couple of U2 tickets for him and, seeing that these were like gold dust, I was about to call in the favour.

I began to explain my predicament. I was frantic, and asked him to help me find the bag. He could see I was not about to take no for an answer, and began to phone around all the probable hotel departments immediately, until he finally traced the journey of my shopping bag. The bag, he explained to me, was now inside an industrial garbage container situated in an alley at the back of the hotel.

With the help of Chris, I began to search the bin for Adam's bag of socks. Only the container was huge, and I had to literally scale the side of it. To keep myself from falling, I had to balance my stomach across the container's rim, while my face and hands were inside the garbage bin, pulling out the stinking bags of rubbish. For almost an hour, Chris and I sifted through the shit, until the bag containing the socks was found.

I knocked at Adam's room, standing there looking very dishevelled, not to mention dirty and smelling of rotten rubbish. My hair was a complete mess, and the clothes I was wearing were completely spoiled. In the process of scaling the container, my stockings had been laddered and my shoes scuffed. But all that mattered was that I had the socks back in my possession.

Adam answered his door wearing some black tracksuit bottoms and a tee shirt. He looked very anxious and teary eyed, like he had been crying. Although I knew I couldn't, I wanted to laugh. It all just seemed surreal.

Adam started to pace the room, asking me accusingly what I had done with his socks. I began to explain what I had done, reminding him that I had now bought him brand new socks. But he was furious with me, demanding to know where his socks were. I offered up the dirty creased bag. Adam snatched it from me, yelling that I was never to dare throw any of his belongings away. As I was about to depart, he said that they were socks from his childhood and he couldn't bear to lose them.

The filming of the *Rattle and Hum* movie meant that there was a film crew and cameras everywhere you went. It was fly-on-the-wall stuff, documenting U2's every move. This had placed not only the band but also its entourage under intense pressure, on top of their already exhausting schedule.

It had also drained my tour budget. I was treading a very fine line between Bono and the tour accountant. In one corner I had the accountant, who was still loath to dish out any extra money towards Bono and the other band members' clothes. He would query every single receipt, dissecting the relative garment's value, as well as questioning whether Bono needed the particular item of clothing in the first place. He was a man good at maths, but when it came to clothes he was clueless.

In the other corner were Bono, Edge, Larry, and Adam, and their personal demands. It wasn't that they needed anything in particular, it was that they wanted to have more designer clothes and expensive toiletries. And what Bono and the band wanted took precedence every time.

A much-repeated request from the boys was for underwear, with all of them requesting specific brands of knickers. Although I would introduce them to various designer clothes, in this particular department they each had their own very precise requirements, and were divided into camps of boxers versus jockeys.

Armed with my shopping list, noting their choices of brands, style and sizes, I went to source their smalls (and, in one case, 'larges').

I thought nothing more about my shopping expedition, until a few days later when a fight broke out between Bono and Larry. There was nothing unusual or ominous to forewarn me of this incident. That particular evening had seen the band perform a brilliant gig, to the delight of the Memphis crowd. The goings-on in the dressing room had so far proved rather uneventful, even though Bono's guests, T. Bone Burnett – who had now made himself almost part of the family, accompanying the band to several of their tour destinations – and the producer Jimmy Iovine, who had been collaborating with Bono on his latest work, had to be ushered from the dressing room. This allowed the boys to prepare themselves for their nightly ablutions, and me to prepare Bono, Larry, Edge and Adam's after-show outfits, including their new knickers.

Larry was the first out of the shower, wrapped in a white bath towel and in a pensive mood, followed by Bono, who was naked, dripping wet, and in high spirits. He was very verbose as he laughed and joked to no one in particular. Calling across the dressing room, he asked me to fetch him some eucalyptus oil, which he had taken to inhaling in the steam of the shower. It helped ease his troubled throat.

As I approached Bono with the oil, Larry, who was towelling himself down, looked across at Bono, who was now stepping into a pair of underpants. The grey jockeys were identical to the ones that I had purchased for Larry, and for some reason this caused Larry to become belligerent. He was like a man possessed. One moment he was quietly drying himself, the next he was waging war over some underpants. Addressing me, he demanded to know what on earth Bono was doing wearing his knickers.

Bono was now seated in his new knickers, paying very little attention to Larry's outburst. Instead, he kept his head down and continued dressing himself, now pulling on some socks, but smirking all the time as he listened to Larry's vitriolic ramblings.

Bono then said to Larry that the underpants weren't exclusive to him (using this comment deliberately, because it was what Larry used to say to Bono all the time).

On hearing this, Larry ceased his vitriol, almost freezing on the spot, as he stood quietly before me, staring at me with a puzzled expression upon his face. Larry was concerned, and needed to know how I could have done such a thing as buy Bono identical knickers. Repeating over and over, he asked me how I could be certain that he would be getting his own underpants back from the wash and not Bono's, adding that there was no way he wanted to wear Bono's underpants.

This made Bono chuckle to himself, but Larry was furious, and what happened next took both Bono and me by surprise. Larry sprang towards Bono, who was still seated, shoving him with such force that he toppled on to the stone floor. A full-on fist fight had now broken out. Bono leapt up on to his feet and retaliated. By this time I did what most girls do when they see men fighting – scream. It wasn't quite Hammer house of horrors, but it was sufficient to bring Adam and Edge, stark bollock naked, from their showers.

Edge and Adam managed to part the warring pair, eventually defusing the situation by asking me what type of knickers I had bought them. They all started laughing. Edge said jokingly to Larry that I was the cause of it all, and therefore should be punished.

I ended up under the shower.

A little shaken by the evening's events (not the fight, but the sight of all those naked men), I was soon being comforted by both Bono and Larry, with Larry apologising for his behaviour and inviting me to dine with him and the other band members, in the hope that some fine food and wine would help resolve The Underpants Dilemma.

I held back my very simple suggestion of sewing name-tags into each of their underpants until after I had eaten. This went down a treat, especially with Bono, who had said earlier that he had no intention of giving up his jockeys.

Chapter 21

Party Pooper Girl

Despite being the most unobtrusive of the band members in many ways, Larry was no pussycat, as his spat with Bono had showed. The incident was, once again, put down to the immense pressure that the band were under due to their increased workload.

The band members' lives at this stage were hectic and arguments were commonplace – not that there was any more fist fighting between them. Still, Larry had further demons to exorcise, as I was about to find out when I accompanied him for a drive.

Larry was not only a Harley Davidson fanatic, but also an avid collector of old jukeboxes and, whatever US state we were in, we would often go shopping, searching out the old junk shops for the machines.

While we were in Miami, Larry had been informed about a particular store on Collins Drive that sold old jukeboxes and, although the band were not encouraged to go anywhere without a minder, they did not always heed the advice. Larry now demonstrated this by asking me to drive him to the store in a two-seater convertible that he had rented.

After finding the store and checking over its merchandise, Larry was hungry and wanted to eat. In our search for a diner, we came across some hard-looking rednecks. They hadn't recognised Larry but, on seeing him with a young woman, had started to wolf whistle at me, adding some lewd remarks to their banter, along with some crude sexual hand gestures. Larry said I was not to pay them any attention and that we should forget about eating and head back to the car.

But I was in a showy-off kind of a mood and, behind Larry's back, without letting him know, I thought I would taunt the bikers with some of my own classic hand signals. My action was not well received. In fact, it had incensed the motley crew, making them want to retaliate with violence towards Larry. The rednecks began to run towards us, yelling out to Larry what they were about to do with him. It sounded nasty. They were, it seemed, ready for the kill.

On hearing the commotion, Larry turned around to see what had irritated the bikers. Seeing them so stirred up and stampeding in our direction panicked him. He grabbed me by the arm as we legged it back to our car.

It was like a scene from a movie as I fumbled nervously with the car keys in an attempt to start the vehicle – hardly the gangster's moll as I hit the pedal to the floor in an attempt to escape our predators. But I had not quite managed to get out of reach of one of the bikers, who lunged manically towards Larry in the passenger seat. Larry's reflexes responded with speed as he swung his legs around the convertible car and aimed them in the direction of his attacker. He then delivered a kung fu-style kick to the lout's chest, sending him flying across the parking lot. With that, I managed to steer the car homeward.

We drove back to our hotel in shocked silence, as my leg quivered about the accelerator pedal, with neither of us quite believing what had taken place. Larry was clearly puzzled by the event and turned around to ask me earnestly, 'Why do you think the bikers got so mad?'

'Gee, I don't know, Larry. They're just a bunch of weirdos.'

Not all of my shopping trips ended up with attempts on my life. This one was an exception, and one that Larry wasn't going to forget in a hurry, saying that in future he was never going to go anywhere without his minder.

It seemed the bigger U2 became the more Mickey Mouse things became, with some major antics filtering down into the band's dressing room.

U2 were playing in Los Angeles, with Los Lobos as their support act. Only Los Lobos hadn't shown up, and there was mass panic backstage. It was only moments before the opening of the gig that we had heard that Los Lobos had been caught up in heavy traffic, and would be late arriving.

This caused some concern with U2's management. Not wanting any ructions from the punters, they were at a loss to know what to do. Jokingly, I said to Bono that he should open his own act. I suggested that I dress him and the band members in some country and western clothes and wigs, disguising them from their fans, so that they could open the gig as some unknown band. Bono loved a prank and was seduced into doing it just for the madness of it all.

I dressed Bono, Edge, Larry and Adam in cowboy hats and waistcoats, even leaving Adam in a pair of his black jogging trousers. This, together with the nasty old wigs, saw them go up on stage introduced as an exciting new country and western act called ''The Dalton Brothers'. They were each introduced to the audience, with Adam being presented as Betty Dalton. It was so funny to stand at the side of stage and watch the faces of the audience as they wondered, is it U2, or isn't it? After a couple of superbly sung country songs, U2 were relieved of their jobs when Los Lobos turned up and scrambled on to the stage to complete their set.

The following day's press had reported the incident under the headline of 'WAS IT OR WASN'T IT?' All the same, The Dalton Brothers received rave reviews. Bono and Edge were so taken with the prank that they got some tee shirts made that had a picture of the U2 band members under the title, 'The Lost Highway Tour'.

This ruse was a one-off, but unfortunately my cock-ups were not.

It was standard procedure that after the soundcheck, with the night's set approved, Joe would hand me a copy of the set list. This enabled me to prepare props, clothing and anything else that might be needed during the course of a show. All the songs on the set list would have been rehearsed at the soundcheck, and then approved by Bono.

I had studied the approved set on this particular day, and noticed that the much-performed, 'Party Girl' song was not in the running. This I found very strange, as U2 were performing at the LA Coliseum in California, with an audience full of famous Hollywood stars. 'Party Girl' was Bono's routine gimmicky number, where he would feign surprise, mid-way through the number, as the bottle of champagne was brought on stage by the beautiful model, or actress, or sometimes by a celebrity's wife. The chosen one would come out from the side of the stage with the champagne and a couple of glasses, and then proceeded to pour Bono and herself a glass.

Bono, Edge and I were seated in the back of a limousine that evening, heading back to the LA stadium in preparation for the night's show, when I mentioned my surprise about the absence of 'Party Girl' from the set list.

However, they paid little attention to what I said.

During this period, Bono had his arm in a sling, nursing

a dislocated collarbone, which he received when falling during a performance back in Canada. But funnily enough he was in good spirits. He was enjoying all the added attention. Everywhere he went, people would fuss over his every whim, myself included. I wasn't complaining because his conviviality was contagious.

The constant attention had made Bono behave like a naughty little schoolboy, going walkabout at the most crucial of moments. This created havoc for me backstage, as he kept disappearing the moment he was left to his own devices – sometimes even in the middle of being dressed. The result was that I would be chasing all over the backstage area of the Coliseum and my work routine was completely thrown off.

That night I had sighed with relief when I heard the thunderous roars of the LA audience as Bono and the band finally stepped on stage. After watching some of the show from the side of the stage, I relaxed a little and continued with my chores back in the dressing room.

It wasn't until I heard the intro to 'Party Girl' fill the dressing room that I suspected anything unusual. Like a Stepford wife, I automatically downed tools and began to run in the direction of the stage, which was quite a way off from the dressing room.

I freaked out, believing that I had fucked up. It was my responsibility to organise all Bono's props, including the champagne. And as I did not have a bottle of champagne ready – and with the name of the person who was meant to take the champagne on stage eluding me – I felt I was done for. I raced towards the side of the stage like a women possessed, holding visions of a ruined career in my mind.

As I was racing along, I tried to remember that night's set list, reassuring myself that the 'Party Girl' song was definitely not on the playlist. I still knew something wasn't right. Only I couldn't work out what it was.

As I frantically came closer to the side of the stage, with my hair and clothes askew, Paul McGuiness stepped in front of me, like he had been waiting for me. He told me that it was imperative that I took the bottle of champagne on stage for Bono, which coincidentally he just happened to have in his hands. Paul's laughter as he, and a couple of crew members, started pushing me towards the side of the stage was a giveaway. Bono, Larry, Edge and Adam had set me up.

But it was too late. Paul ignored my resistant pleas and shoved me on stage.

Bono had often asked me to come on stage with the champagne, to which I replied by just laughing and telling him that there was no chance, that pigs had more chance of flying, and that I was definitely 'a behind the scenes kinda gal'.

And here I was, on stage in front of 80,000 people, looking like I had been dragged through a hedge backwards. I couldn't have been more mortified.

I don't think anybody could have foreseen the outcome

of the boys' prank. Getting me on that stage seriously backfired on them, and turn a U2 gig into a Laurel and Hardy-style farce. Because I came stumbling on to the stage having been pushed, I had to regain my balance. This had shaken up the champagne bottle which I was holding as I meekly aimed my body and the bottle towards Bono, who was at the front of stage singing into his mike.

He had not noticed me approaching as I sneaked up on him, lifting my leg as I got closer, in order to try and playfully kick him in the arse. But, at that exact moment, he had turned his body towards me, and my foot connected with his bollocks, which obviously caused him some discomfort and made him clutch at his manhood with his free hand (the other being in a sling). Just then, the champagne cork decided to flew off directly into his forehead, sending the fizz spraying into his eyes.

By this time, there wasn't a dry eye in the house, as the auditorium broke into hysterical laughter. It was pandemonium. Larry, Edge and Adam were in hysterics as they went to check on Bono, who was now bent down on his knees, keeled over, not quite sure whether to laugh or cry. He stayed in that position, milking it for all it was worth, for what seemed like an eternity.

I fled the stage. Even though Edge tried to make it better as I exited, I was inconsolable. The havoc that I had just wreaked on U2 left me deeply embarrassed, and I had wanted to run right away, but, the very next moment, I heard Bono telling the audience that he loved Lola, and he was beckoning me back on stage. 'Lola, I love you. Come back, girl, bring on the champagne,' he was now shouting into his microphone. And the audience now accompanied him, chanting for me to reappear.

Getting back on that stage did not bear thinking about, but it happened. Once again the crew lifted me up and placed me on stage, dumbfounded. I'm not quite sure what took place from that moment on as fear erased the memory. But the sound of 80,000 people laughing still haunts me to this day.

Chapter 22

Film Stars Behaving Badly

I would like to say that the rest of the tour went without a hitch, but that was not the case. It was a constant source of amazement to me when I saw Bono finally step on stage. I would sigh with relief, and even giggle to myself, as he appeared in the spotlight to the adulation of his adoring public, who could not possibly have suspected some of the catastrophes that had occurred behind the scenes.

The stage was possibly Bono's safest haven.

A lot of the calamities that happened during the tour were not caused by Bono, but he could, at times, help matters along. This was especially true the time he encouraged Faye Dunaway's sympathy for his already healing collarbone.

The dressing room is an area that was totally out of bounds, except for the band, the band's manager, and the band members' invited guests. This restriction included staff and family. With so much of their private time spent in the dressing room, it really was the inner sanctum. An invitation into the dressing room was a real compliment.

One particular night we were still at the LA Stadium and, prior to the band's performance, Bono was entertaining and holding court to Faye Dunaway and his very close friend Gavin Friday. Copious amounts of booze were being downed and, with Bono still suffering some discomfort from his dislocated collarbone, he was milking the situation like only Bono could, especially with Faye busily fluffing around him, barking orders at Gavin and myself, sending us backwards and forwards to fetch ice for Bono's injury. As for Bono, he was sitting back enjoying every minute of it.

As the evening's gig drew near, I asked everyone in the room to leave, allowing me time to prepare Bono and the boys for their show. Only Faye was not budging. She insisted on staying put, even after Gavin's kind offer to escort her to the nearest watering hole. With time running out, we had all become very agitated, Bono included, who began eyeing me anxiously in the hope that I could free him.

But this was no easy task. Faye had firmly attached herself to Bono. She was seated beside him, applying ice, which she had wrapped in a towel, to his injured shoulder, ignoring all requests for her to leave.

Heads held high, beaming white teeth spread across smiling faces, was the usual look of the stars as they gained their coveted audience with Bono inside his dressing room. But this did not necessarily guarantee them the same passage out. Still, I don't think anybody could have predicted the fate that would befall Jack Nicholson.

Jack was a huge fan of Bono, and had attended a lot of U2 gigs. On the whole, his behaviour backstage was nothing but gentlemanly. But, one particular night, Jack was acting very strangely. He had been invited back to Bono's dressing room prior to U2's final performance in the LA Stadium, and he was giving Bono some cause for concern – to the extent that Bono called on me for a favour.

When I asked what favour he had in mind – thinking it might be something to do with his notepads, which he was forever losing and had started handing over to me for safekeeping – he asked me to babysit Jack Nicholson. He needed me to keep an eye on him, he said.

This request had made me very nervous. When he elaborated, telling me that I had to keep Jack from watching the show from the side of the stage, as is normal for a lot of privileged guests, I thought Bono was not quite the ticket himself. In fact, I thought he was crazy. And it made me panicky. Bono was undeterred by my resistance.

Jack had been sitting in Bono's dressing room apparently in tears. Bono had said to me that he felt awkward, and wasn't sure what to say to Jack, or do, to console him. Everyone in the dressing room had been embarrassed.

But I didn't want to be involved with Bono's scheme. Me, babysitting Jack Nicholson? It was ludicrous. I laughed out loud at the thought, and told Bono that I couldn't do it, adding, 'What am I supposed to speak to him about?' I then went into a sarcastic dialogue saying, 'Hi, Jack, my name's Lola, and I will be your prison warder for the night.'

Just because nobody else knew what to do for him, I thought it unfair to leave him with me. But that was just what happened – with Bono fearing, he said, that Jack was so off his face he might step on stage.

'Lola, you have to do this for me,' he insisted, 'and be discreet.' With that, Bono, Larry, Edge and Adam, along with their tour manager, left the dressing room and headed towards the stage and their night's performance. And me? I was left trembling, ready to begin my own night's performance.

Jack was sombre when I approached him. That I had been instructed by Bono not to take my eyes off of him amused me because, whenever he was on a movie screen, I couldn't. But I had ignored Bono's instructions on this particular night, leaving the room only in order to top up my lipstick and powder my nose. I thought to myself that even if Jack was a little out of his box, he would appreciate my effort. My night with Jack Nicholson was one I will always remember, even though Jack would have been hard pressed to remember his own name.

We sat on one of the wooden benches which were scattered about the backstage hospitality area. It was now empty of guests. They were all out at the front of stage watching the show.

It was so surreal, sitting under a Californian sky with Jack Nicholson. He was talking about the wonders of the universe and, all the time I was listening, Bono and U2 were playing in the background. He began to cry, sitting there, just staring up at the night sky. He said to me that his tears were because he'd had a realisation: that all he ever wanted to be was Jack Nicholson. I wasn't sure what he meant, but supposed that being out of his head was some kind of release from all the Hollywood pretension.

My date with Jack Nicholson was cut short as soon as the gig was over. I kissed his wet cheek, and wished him well. I was gutted he didn't ask for my telephone number. I'm sure it was a mere oversight.

Chapter 23

When Love Almost Left Town

The entourage was on the move again. This time we were heading out from LA on to quieter pastures, or at least that was what I was hoping for in Missouri: Middle America – The Gateway to the West. St Louis – what exciting images that evoked for me, thanks to Judy Garland, and her song 'Meet Me In St Louis'. Annoyingly, I was humming the tune all morning.

Although LA had seen U2 play some spectacular gigs, the backstage events had been anything but successful. Most of my time had been spent with my heart in my mouth. And, with one too many cock-ups having occurred for my liking, I had requested that I fly out ahead of the band.

It is true that one should expect nothing – that way, you

can never be disappointed. St Louis was not all that I hoped it would be. In fact, staying at the hotel was like living in a shopping mall. The hotel corridors, depressingly, overlooked the bustling shoppers, and muzak wafted through the entire hotel, even into your room. I was feeling depressed and lonely.

I left my luggage in the hotel room, and requested a car and driver from Theresa. A colleague of mine back home in England had informed me that there were many second-hand clothes shops throughout Middle America. She had enthused about their brilliance, emphasising the fact that some unique items could be found in them. With that in mind, I asked the driver to take me to an area renowned for such shops.

A gleaming white stretch limousine was placed at my disposal. To say this brought me a lot of attention is an understatement. St Louis is not known as the most affluent of American states. Nor was the area I was being driven into a particularly safe one.

The first thing that struck me as we approached the downtown neighbourhood was the poverty. The sidewalk was relatively free of folk, except for a few down-and-outs, and they looked mean. As we neared my destination, I became quite nervous about leaving the safety of the car, especially as the people had now stopped in their tracks and were eyeing it. I asked the driver to park a little way ahead of the shops but, by doing so, felt I was compromising my safety. Having given myself a peptalk, telling myself over and over, 'I can do this,' I stepped out of the car, reminding myself how good I was at running. I told the driver to tell my mom I forgive her if I wasn't back within the hour.

I then made my way down the street. I walked the walk, holding myself erect as I strode along the sidewalk, acting like I was born on the streets of Missouri. Only I wasn't and I was shitting myself.

Once inside the shop, I was left to my own devices, perhaps because the owner thought I had lost my marbles. Most strangers wouldn't dare frequent such a neighbourhood. This was the type of shop that mainly serviced the surrounding housing projects. It could have been just the way the old man in the store did things, but I was not spoken to.

I browsed the racks and shelves of this wonderful old shop, finding and buying up clothes that I felt could be brought back to life. Some pinstriped jackets had taken my fancy, and some unusual-cut trousers also caught my eye. These, along with a cravat and an old harmonica, which I bought with Bono in mind, made the day a success.

Although I had had been lost in my own little world as I searched the shop for hidden treasure, I was now very self-conscious about searching through my bag for my purse. Feeling slightly paranoid, and not wanting any of the other shoppers to notice my wallet, which was stuffed full of cash, I fumbled about surreptitiously inside my handbag to extract the dollars from my wallet. In the process, I had to empty some of the paraphernalia from the inside my bag on to one of the counters.

I paid cash for my purchases and, as this was clearly not the kind of shop that sold large quantities of stock, they had no shopping bags. Still not wanting any unnecessary attention, I offered no complaints. I left the store looking like a bag lady myself, as I struggled along the sidewalk – now not so much walking the walk as juggling the juggle, as I desperately sought to balance all my items.

I was safely back at my hotel when I discovered what I felt sure was to be my final mistake with U2. I had lost Bono's notepad. And this was no ordinary notepad. It was one of the five that I had found hidden at the back of Bono's wardrobe trunk at the start of my job. He was so delighted to be reunited with the yellow notepads, and his earlier scribbling, that it inspired him, or so he told me, to rework some of the lyrics in this particular pad. He had read me some of the lines to the start of a new song that he said he was rewriting especially with BB King in mind.

What was I to do? It was eventually recorder as 'When Love Comes to Town'. He had given me the notepad to look after because he was always losing or misplacing them. And now I had done exactly the same. I was panic-stricken, holding my hands to my head as I tried to gather my thoughts. Shit! I was doomed.

Not trusting my own judgement, I once again searched

through my handbag, as well as checking through the assortment of newly purchased clothes, in the faint hope that the pad would be found among them. But it wasn't. The only hope left was to go back to the store to see if it was there.

For somebody who had not wanted to bring attention to themselves I was now doing a terrific job. Turning up twice in a day in a neighbourhood that was not often frequented by strangers was one thing, but to show up in the flashiest of vehicles was asking for trouble.

Entering the old man's shop for a second time in a day made him very suspicious of me – and talkative. He wanted to know what it was that I was looking for. He watched me as I searched frantically through his junk shop. I told him that I had lost my notepad, and that it was important I find it. And, just as I was describing it to him, it turned up. It had been lying amongst some useless-looking items on the counter.

I was delighted to be reunited with the little yellow pad, and told the shopkeeper several times how grateful I was to have found it. This obviously sent alarm bells ringing in his head. Because he was not prepared to let me leave his shop until I had paid good money for that little pad.

The foxy old man ignored all my protestations that the notepad was my lost property. And he made it very clear that it was not for sale unless a good price was agreed.

And so my misfortune became his good fortune.

Chapter 24

Antoine's Bar, Texas

While U2 were travelling, like Roman centurions conquering their way through different towns and countries, I tried to make a point of visiting places of interest in each town we were in. Perhaps I would take advantage of a museum or an art gallery. But, as we were in Texas, with the shops full of authentic country and western dress, I did what I did best – shopped. And with Bono and Edge both great admirers of western-style clothes, I wasted no time. In fact, they had both given me shopping lists of gifts and things that they wanted, along with very clear instructions to buy them authentic cowboy boots, shirts and hats. There were plenty of stores displaying such wares, and I found myself spoilt for choice.

The day was pretty eventful, if only because I bought so many things. Adam had whinged that he felt left out, with country and western clothes not being to his liking, but there was not much I could do about it. I consoled him with an old Muddy Waters CD that I found along the way.

The night's gig went without any hitches. But, before the show began, Bono's dressing room was holding its own little performance. Although it was part of my responsibility to empty the dressing room of guests well in advance of the night's gig, on this particular night, for my own selfish reasons, I didn't.

While I had been dressing Bono and the boys, they had been talking music with their guests, who were the actor Harry Dean Stanton (who was in the movie *Paris, Texas*) and T. Bone Burnett. They had become pretty passionate about things, everyone talking over each other and wanting to prove their musical points. When Harry Dean asked Bono if he could play his guitar, which was lying nearby on the sofa, Bono agreed, and handed it over to him. Harry Dean then sat back on the sofa, strumming a tune, with Bono sitting on the arm of a chair opposite, accompanying the guitar with a harmonica that he had tucked into his waistcoat pocket. T. Bone was standing by the two of them, shaking a tambourine that had also been lying about the dressing room. They all began to improvise, playing and singing aloud, making up the rhymes and rhythms as they went along. The atmosphere in the small backstage dressing room was just amazing – and they were all lost in the moment.

To have been fortunate enough to witness such a rare event was extremely moving. The music that was spontaneously resonating from the grungy old room sent goosebumps down the length of my spine. What I saw and heard that night was magical. It was one of those very special moments that occur by chance, once in a blue moon.

And all that wonderful conviviality continued through the evening. Even after Bono had completed his show, he was still buzzing with excitement. And when T. Bone suggested that we all go on to Antoine's Bar – an apparently renowned blues bar in downtown Houston – Bono agreed without hesitation, organising the whole thing right down to arranging the transport and inviting me and Finton along.

Bono was on a roll that night, saying that he felt out of this world. I didn't think he was capable of getting any higher but, on learning that Stevie Ray Vaughan and his brother were playing in the bar that night, his energy soared even higher.

Antoine's Bar was heaving.

I don't know if it was Bono's energy or his friend's enthusiasm, or a combination of the two, but the night was filled with electricity. Sparks were flying.

T. Bone, being the tallest of our party at 6ft, had spotted some people about to vacate a table, and had manoeuvred his way through the crowd. We all followed, with Bono 'hidden' in among us, as we jostled through a sea of people, eventually seating ourselves around the large wooden table.

The crowd eventually started to realise who had arrived, and now and then a fan would approach the table requesting Bono's autograph. He duly obliged, instructing John, his minder, to let the fans come near.

Stevie Ray Vaughan took to the stage with his brother, and they let rip, with the sound from their electric guitars engulfing what felt like the whole of Houston. Everybody in the bar was blown by the sound of the music generating from that small platform.

Bono and T. Bone got up from the table and walked towards the mezzanine in order to pay their respects to Stevie and his brother, but Stevie insisted that they get up on stage and play a number. So that night saw another impromptu performance from Bono and T. Bone, this time with the Vaughan brothers. The crowd in the bar was totally silenced.

The party was now in full flow, with everybody going for it, drinking and dancing to the sound of the blues. But Bono's mischief wasn't over yet. We were seated around our wooden table once more, when a couple of young girls approached. They wanted Bono's autograph and he was only too willing to oblige. As he was in the process of signing the young brunette's photograph, she mentioned that she too was a musician: a classical pianist. Bono teased her by saying that he didn't believe her, and that if she really was, she was to go up on stage and play something. The young girl declined, saying that the piano up on the platform was not tuned correctly, and that it would not be suitable for her to play on. With that, she addressed Bono quite boldly, saying, 'But you could come back to my house and I will play you something on my own piano.'

Bono did not need more of a dare, and he rose to the bait, asking, 'Can my friends come, too?'

The young girls were astounded by Bono's acceptance, and began squealing and dancing about the floor. Wasting no time, Bono quickly added, 'How do we get there?' Politely refusing her other offer of a ride in her car, Bono told her that she should drive her car in front of his limousine, and that we would follow her. This she did and, true to his word, Bono, his minder, T. Bone, Harry Dean, Finton and I all followed her car in the gleaming white stretch limo.

When we arrived at the wooden weather-boarded house, she invited us in.

In the limo we had been teasing Bono, saying he was old-fashioned for having to take us all along on his date.

The little wooden house was too small to accommodate us all comfortably, so the porch door was left ajar. Bono's minder perched himself there like a bird of prey, watching over the whole spectacle.

As we entered, the first thing we noticed was a very

beautiful Steinway piano. And on the stool of the piano seat sat a pile of dirty washing. In fact, the entire house could have been mistaken for a Chinese laundry.

True enough, the lively young girl was, as she had said, a musician. She sat at her piano and played a small recital of classics. Then, without warning, she burst into a rendition of 'With or Without You' at which point Bono joined her, with the rest of us singing along. After she had finished, we all cheered and applauded her efforts. Then, after a few exchanges of banter between her and Bono, we left as we arrived – noisily – and headed back to the hotel.

In the back of the limousine, Bono said that he felt 'so sorry for the young girl'. Laughing at the thought of her telling her mates, he added, 'Who on earth is going to believe her story?'

Chapter 25

A Conspiracy of Hope

It was evident that U2 and their organisation were paranoid about letting outsiders in. And, no matter how hard I tried to endear myself to Ellen and co. for the sake of professionalism, I was never really accepted. As far as she and Principal Management were concerned, I was an outsider, and that was how it would remain.

Many a night saw me lying awake, trying to work out why, but the answer always eluded me. With Bono's attention almost always at my command, solely through the nature of my job, I was deemed a threat. But I was determined that I was going nowhere. Well, at least not until the end of tour.

The tour was nearing its end, and U2, with their extremely large entourage, were finally descending upon

Phoenix Arizona in order to play their farewell gig. I had wanted to have fun. And what better way to enjoy myself, I thought, than to invite Peter and Michael out to join me.

The past four months had been intense, making it seem more like four years. Phil Janou and his film crew had been closely documenting Bono and the band's every move with a handheld camera. They had shot untold amounts of film footage in their attempt to make the *Rattle and Hum* movie.

All the band members had become jumpy, and were now starting to fret about having allowed Phil Janou so much access to them. Phil had been privy to a lot of the band's partying, including days going by without some of them even sleeping. McGuiness assured them that they had nothing to worry about, and that Principal Management had complete control of all the film that had been taken.

Bono, Larry, Edge and Adam were all being very secretive, even among themselves. I was forever being sworn to secrecy by individual band members, sometimes for what felt like the silliest of reasons. It was nervewracking for me having to be the keeper of so many of their clandestine dealings. Everything, it seemed, in the world of Bono, U2 and their management company was hush-hush.

Bono loved and often quoted the phrase 'A Conspiracy

of Hope'. 'It's whatever you do, if you can just do it with a bit of dignity.' He added that he hoped it could be used to describe all that U2 and their organisation stood for.

But it was not necessarily the belief of his manager, or the rest of the honchos at Principal Management. And these were the people that surrounded him

Paul McGuiness was U2's hard-nosed manager. The music industry has always been renowned for its manipulative managers. It is a very tough, competitive industry. To be able to survive in it, one had to be resilient as well as dedicated. It was a well-known fact, in that world, that belonging to a band that had a great sound and image did not necessarily guarantee success. Having a tough, shrewd, and in some cases uncomprimising negotiator at the helm did.

McGuiness's reputation preceded him. He was known as a formidable businessman, and it had often been said that Bono, and U2, would not be where they were – even with their brilliant sound – without such a strong and hard-nosed character for a manager.

In developing and selling artists, the music manager's role is paramount. It is make or break. And often, in the pursuit of stardom, musicians are prepared to sit back and let the managers get on with what is the sometimes messy work of promoting them.

Just as Bono and U2 stood at the pinnacle of their profession, with virtually every music award to their name as proof, McGuiness stood at the pinnacle of his.

And, even though they don't have awards and ceremonies in recognition of proud, hard-nosed managers, if they did, he would be the uncontested champion. For in his line of business, rotund and balding McGuiness clearly outshone his peers. He stood on his own podium.

By the late 1980s, having helped Bono and U2 achieve such great success, McGuiness was now buying up most of the run-down areas of Dublin on behalf of himself and the band. Paul was keen to invest his and U2's wealth, and advised Bono that one of the best investments they could make was to buy up the dockland area around the Liffey, which McGuiness had informed Bono could be picked up really cheaply. Paul had mentioned that the land was ripe for development. He also emphasised that it would reap them huge financial gain.

But Bono was hesitant, airings his reservations by saying that he did not want to rush into making any decisions. He was concerned about how it would appear to U2 fans if they found out how wealthy he was.

But the other band members didn't agree. Adam stated that he did not give a fuck what anyone thought, adding that he could do whatever he liked with his money. He had partied hard for it. Larry agreed, but along with Edge was on the side of caution.

In reply to Bono's concerns about buying the docklands, Paul said that the land could be used to build U2's new recording studios, or some other related project.

Therefore it would not look like a blatant investment. On hearing that, Bono gave his endorsement.

These money talks in dressing rooms had started to become a regular occurrence.

During the late afternoon, Bono and the band members would be at whatever venue they were playing, in order to run through their soundcheck. Only the soundcheck had become known among the crew as 'money check', with rehearsals frequently held up while McGuiness thrashed out these other business dealings with the boys. The band had to agree unanimously on any decisions that were taken. U2's contract was split five ways, with McGuiness the fifth band member.

Bono was contrary, and he knew it. Being a rock star who was not only loaded but had also gained world recognition was of great comfort to him. He had relentlessly pursued fame and glory, and was now reaping the rewards: money and adulation.

But Bono did not want to appear to be one of the owning classes. Although he had succumbed to the rock'n'roll lifestyle, he was anxious to still be seen by his public as a regular Joe.

Once again the result was Bono battling with himself.

He still hadn't found what he was looking for: reconciliation.

I know, as I sit here writing this, that many things I once dreamt of and desired are no longer meaningful to me. And so it is, I'm sure, for all of us. Even Bono. We all grow and change as human beings. Beliefs we held yesterday may no longer apply today.

I have always lived my life on the edge. I knew from a very early age that a nine-to-five existence was not going to do it for me – and I never sought it. I often suspect my father's bohemian influence rubbed off on me. This has sometimes been to my cost. Working freelance means that, once your last project is over, you are never quite sure where the next job is coming from. Of course, sometimes I have been very fortunate, seeing myself booked up for months ahead with project after project. But after every feast comes the famine.

At the end of the *Joshua Tree* and *Rattle and Hum* tours, I was – to my surprise – asked by Paul McGuiness to stay on permanently and work solely for Bono and U2. But, even with the tempting offer of a large retainer, I refused. Surprisingly, it was not a difficult decision for me to make. I felt I was just not a strong enough person to deal with the internal politics of Principal Management, and besides I still possessed a few brain cells. I needed to be happy in my work. It was as pure and simple as that, and any more time spent among them would have made me feel like I was doing time!

Bono's redeeming features did not outweigh those of his management, and the thought of having to spend any more of my time avoiding landmines did not appeal. In fact, it exhausted me.

Ellen was relentless and wanted me out, and, as she

had pointed out to me months earlier, Bono would not be able to save me, and he and I knew it. He had asked me to forgive his selfishness as he tried hard to persuade me to stay on, thinking up various scenarios that could make the situation easier.

My final departure from Larry, Adam and Edge was a bit like my entrance into their world at the start of the tour: silent. This was partly due to the fact that, by the time I had made my decision to leave, the boys had already flown home to Ireland.

The last words Bono said to me, when he knew my mind was set, were, 'Lola, I love you. You gave me clothes that kept me warm on the inside.'

And for me that was the greatest reward of all.

Chapter 26

Epilogue

I was a freelancer. Like most of the people who make up the workforce in the music industry, we go in, apply ourselves to a project for however long it takes, and then we leave. This had always suited me. Especially as some things never change, such as my dislike of being told what to do.

It is still amazing to me how people come and go from our lives so easily. One moment you're a close family, the next you're a lone soldier; but that's life and never more true than with life on the road.

It was not too long before I was rockin'n'rollin again – only this time it was with a very different family. One that was warm and intimate. George Michael's band and entourage travelled lightly, not taking themselves at all seriously. What surprised me was just how supportive his entire crew and management were.

Work had now taken a more relaxed and, dare I say it, fun turn.

George wanted me to create him an image for his upcoming *Faith* tour. This was to be the last tour George would do for years. Although none of us knew it at the time, he was soon to enter into a very public battle with his music label, Sony.

The *Faith* tour was not without its own madness, and one of my more outstanding recollections of this particular time was when the entire band and I were taken at gunpoint from a restaurant down at the marina of Porta Banus, Spain. There had been some misunderstanding with the Spanish Government as to what time, or whether, George would go on stage and perform, and with it being a huge outdoor event, the Spanish police panicked, fearing a riot. To secure some bargaining power, they held George's musicians and me as pawns until the negotiations – backwards and forwards – between them and George's management had been settled.

Seeking adventure and a nonconformist lifestyle had its own joys. But never knowing where your next pound was coming from didn't make for an easy life. It seemed that I enjoyed the trauma of not knowing what was next – not that I would want to change a thing from my past. I feel so fortunate to have had the opportunities I've had.

Having spent the last four years of my life between England and Australia has changed me completely. I can now appreciate the things that make for a very simple life. The excitement of clubs and stadiums that I once yearned for and loved so much have been swapped for greener pastures. Designer shops I exchanged for … well, designer shops. I haven't completely lost my mind!

Living in the outback of Australia, on a friend's remote cattle station, was always going to challenge me. Which was exactly what I needed. I wanted to find out who I was, and what it was that I would do next. After having had such an incredibly exciting career, the thought of my next journey was frightening. But I wanted to move on and, more importantly, I wanted to face my fears – and boy were there a lot of them.

Australia was going to be the place where I confronted them.

Over the years I have spent a lot of my time with close friends on their remote property in Queensland, Australia. Inevitability, with so much of my time spent there, I learnt the ways of the land, along with many farming skills, which Gavin, a close friend, taught me. This in itself was unbelievable, especially since I was equipped with only manicured nails and an urban background to rely on. But the fact that I was terrified of spiders, and still managed to live on a property that was going to bring me into daily contact with them was, to me, bloody amazing.

Somebody had once asked me if I was afraid of snakes. I laughed into my cocktail, and replied, 'I live in the city. Why on earth should I be afraid of snakes?' That amuses me now. Yes, I am fucking terrified of them, and Queensland is home to nine of the deadliest snakes in the world.

The other great learning curve for me was the fact that the good old Aussies don't give a fuck about who you are, or what you are. They only care about what you can do. And now I was leaving Queensland, and Gavin, for one of the remotest cattle stations, in Western Australia, where there was a lot of doing to be done.

Finally arriving at Bedford Down's cattle station, I was overwhelmed by its beauty. In fact, the whole region in which it is situated, 'The Kimberleys', is truly magnificent. I had always thought of Ireland, with its forty shades of green, as God's country – but now I know different.

With the Kimberleys' monsoon-like climate, most of the cattle work took place from March through to the end of August. By the end of the season, the rains fell so hard that they flooded most of the land in the region, making it impossible to work, and sometimes for the residents to even live there.

For quite some time, I had been nagging away at my dear friends Sal and Jim Renshaw, asking them to allow me to help out on their land, but there was little to do on their property. So Sal suggested that I go out and experience working on a big cattle station. She even helped me to find the work.

Like everything, it's not what you know, but who you know, and with Sal and Jim coming from a well-respected agricultural family they had many contacts around Australia. One of them eventually offered me a position.

Now I am no Jamie Oliver or Nigella, but I love to cook, and it was no hardship when I was told that I had secured the job as station cook at the Bedford Downs Cattle Station, W.A. Cooking for cowboys. Hmm, I thought. This could be interesting.

Only when I arrived at the station, during the wee hours of the morning, having journeyed for almost a week, in the front of one of the Frank Blinco road trains, was I informed that my position had now changed. I had been promoted – to stock-camp cook. Somehow, this did not sound good.

For starters, I had never heard of a stock-camp cook and, second, I had no idea what I was meant to do. But Sterling Buntine, the owner of the station, had no problem instructing me, adding it would take him a day to show me. I was absolutely horrified, especially when he described the running of a cattle station. But, whether I liked it or not, I was stuck with it.

I had thought that my duties would involve cooking for cowboys in the cattle station's kitchen, and cattle station kitchens were renowned throughout Australia for being professionally designed and run. A lot of them were run just like restaurants, so my friend the famous Australian chef Chrissie Mansfield had told me, even handing me one of her cookbooks for assistance.

In my free time, I was told, I would be helping the ringers down at the cattle yards, which involved being on horseback, which I love, and working among the cattle branding and mustering, which I grew to love.

But no, there was no restaurant kitchen where I was going. There wasn't even a building! But there were plenty of horses and cattle and dingoes – and, if that wasn't enough, deadly snakes and crocodiles. Along with plenty of vast open spaces.

There was no way to get off, from Bedford Downs, until the next road trains which would come to collect the cattle. And that was months away, as Sterling had very kindly pointed out to me.

The Kimberlys was a vast, rugged region of Western Australia. The Flinders were the lower mountain ranges that surrounded the cattle station. They provided a constant supply of water, vital for breeding cattle. And being able to depend on a constant source, thanks to the lie of the land, had helped the region to become known for having some of the finest beef herds in Australia. This made the area rich, and their owners richer – they supplied a lot of Japan and the Far East with their prime meat.

Other than via helicopter or road train, there was no way in or out of Bedford Downs, unless you had a four-wheel drive – which I didn't. But there was no use crying, I had to get on with it, and get on with I did.

There was definitely no point in trying to explain to Buntine that I had never lived outside in the open, let alone cooked outside. I didn't even know how to use a barbeque.

My duties were to cook for 16 ringers, otherwise known as cowboys. These cowboys kept the station running. Their duties consisted of finding the various herds of cattle that were allowed to roam freely across the land, be they wild bulls or heifers. Then, upon finding the specific herd, they would muster them back into the cattle yards, which they also had to erect, if the cattle had been spotted far away. Most of their work was done on horseback, although, with the station covering an area almost the size of England, a helicopter was often needed for assistance.

Once the beasts had been rounded up into the makeshift holdings, they had to be drafted into various other holdings. Which holding depended on factors such as the size and quality of the animal. Some of the injured or not too kosher-looking cattle ended up as hamburger meat.

In order for me to do my job, I had to learn to cook over an open fire that I had to learn to make. I also had to load a caravan, which took the place of a larder, full of stores. The food supplies consisted mainly of an assortment of tinned foods, and fresh vegetables or fruit, plus tea, sugar, powdered milk and condiments. Once all this had been organised, my caravan-cum-kitchen was stocked.

Inside the grungy old caravan-trailer was a trunk filled with billycans and other useful cooking utensils. The blacked up, fire-burnt billycans were used in place of regular saucepans and frying pans. There was also a tiny little fridge that ran off a generator that used fuel. But it hardly worked, as it was always running out of juice.

Once the caravan-trailer was stocked, I was then given instructions on how to tow it out into what seemed like the middle of nowhere. And, try as I might to tell Sterling that I had never, ever towed a vehicle in my life – least of all across such rugged landscape, it all fell on deaf ears. This was a hardcore Northern Territory man.

All he ever said was, 'You can do it.'

How do I try to explain the fear and trepidation that I first felt when getting behind the wheel of the Ute with a caravan to tow, and no idea where I was heading?

I hadn't really understood Sterling's directions, but felt I couldn't ask him to explain them again. He had repeated the directions to me four times already. His instructions were along the lines of, 'Go thirty kilometres along the dirt track …' (It all looked like dirt track, and what were kilometres?) '… then, on approaching the white gate, turn off to the left …' (Was that after I went through it or before?) '… Keep going until you come across a Pandana tree …' (What the fuck was a Pandana tree?) ' … then motor for another 30ks, until you came across some creeks. Go across both the creeks …' (These looked like fucking rivers, he had to be joking.) And so it went on.

Yes, I did fuck up. No, I never found my way, and, yes, Sterling would have had me off his property if he could have found another person crazy enough to undertake such a job. Did I mention there were crocodiles in the creeks?

As the weeks went by, I became a bit of a dab hand at cooking over the open fire, and with the temperature sometimes reaching up into the 40s, I truly understood the expression 'slaving over a hot stove'!

Some of the Aboriginal ringers, who I was cooking for, began to teach me how to build a fire. I wasn't sure if it was a show of friendship or that they wanted to make sure they had their grub.

The boys pointed out to me the appropriate woods to cook with. They taught me the different value of each of the various gum tree barks, showing me the ones that burnt slower than the others. The slower-burning barks would eventually break down into hot coals, which could be used for a variety of things. But mostly it was sought for slow baking. This was a very traditional way of cooking in the out bush, and was achieved by burying the cooking pot in the ground, then covering it with the hot coals, until the food was baked. There was no way to preserve the food, and this meant you could leave the food cooking slowly for most of the day just by topping up the coals.

The ringers also showed me the bark needed to get a fire started very quickly. They explained that the skinny bark of the snappy gum tree was the usual choice. You peeled off any of the dried leaves attached and placed them in a mould-like fashion underneath the bark. This helped them light even quicker.

Sleeping out under the stars of those big Australian skies was addictive, even though my sleeping took place in the back of the open Ute. At the end of each evening, I would clear everything from the back of the truck – saddles and bridles, and other paraphernalia. With clearing and putting away all the cooking utensils out of the way, I would prepare for bed – a swag bag that I unrolled on to the floor of the Ute – taking extra precautions never to take my eyes of it for a minute to avoid any snakes getting inside, which had been known to happen. The ringers all unrolled their swag around the campfire, just like you see in the cowboy movies. And usually, as soon as their heads hit their pillows, they were out, and the night was silent. Except for the nights when we would hear the blood-curdling howls of the wild dingoes, which would surround the camp in search of food.

At first I thought I would die with fright, thinking that if a snake didn't get me the dingoes would. And it was of no use telling the men how scared I was, as they would just have used this as an excuse to scare you even more. Having said all that, I long for the chance to do it all again. Even though my time out bush was not easy, I loved every single minute of it.

I would be up at some ridiculous hour, even by my

standards. I am a naturally early riser, but 3am was a little early even for me.

Once up, and armed with my new-found knowledge of fire making, I would throw the snappy bark on to the paper, which I lit with the help of some matches. With the fire burning I then added the heavier gum bark in preparation for cooking the cowboys' breakfast – a full-on meat dish. This was usually a stew, which had been prepared at the end of the previous day. With no refrigeration to speak of, I had to be very careful how I used the food. Most of the dishes consisted mainly of meat. It was, after all, a cattle station, with a 40,000 herd of prime beef. The cowboys were laughing – steak every day. Only I was vegetarian.

I have never met a harder-working bunch of people than the Aussies. But the bushmen and cowboys, who work out on the cattle stations and properties, win all the prizes, along with my admiration. They work long and hard, with most of the Aboriginal ringers having known no other life.

I became known among the men as Cookie and, although it was unoriginal, I thought it rather endearing. Cookie, at times, amazed herself, delivering up good, hot food – meals that were openly appreciated by each of the cowboys. I had even learnt to make fresh bread, known out in the bush as 'damper'. This I would bake in the earth. There wasn't much apart from food for the ringers to look forward to after a hard day's graft. And being a dry station (no alcohol was allowed), it gave me great pleasure to conjure up a rich variety of dishes to set before my cowboys.

With Bedford Downs being so vast, and spread across so much rugged terrain, it was impossible to cover the land other than on horseback. And to find the cattle solely on horseback would take many months. The only other solution was helicopter. The cowboys would have to take instruction from Sterling on where to find the cattle. Sterling would gather this information by air. He was a licensed muster pilot, which allowed him to fly low over the land (this is a very dangerous thing to do, and takes a lot of skill) in order to find his herd. Once he spotted the beasts, he would radio their whereabouts to his head ringer who was waiting by a two-way radio, inside one of the air-conditioned vehicles. The head ringer would then drive out to the other cowboys who were back at the makeshift cattle yards, to inform them of his news. Depending on how far off the herd was spotted, the boys would then saddle up, and head out in the direction of the cattle. This could take weeks. It all depended on the size of the herd and its location.

In the meantime, I would have to drive the truck that towed the caravan trailer out to any given location, in order to be near the men. Once I actually located the place, it was imperative that I find a shady location in which to park the Ute and trailer. This was sometimes a tall order given the temperatures. After this, I would start preparing the camp. The first thing was to get a fire going, then collect the water and wood, in order to start on the cooking. This had to be done well in advance of the cowboys' arrival. When they arrived they were starving.

None of this was an easy task, especially the drive. I swear some of the land I drove across had never encountered a human before. I was forever getting lost, although I was told repeatedly by Sterling that it was impossible. It was just rugged wilderness of bush out there. Mostly dense and hidden, with skinny gum trees, bushes and rocky boulders to drive through.

Sterling would scream, shout and swear at me every time I fucked up and had to radio him on the two-way to come and rescue me. He would fly over the land in his helicopter searching for me, often amazed that I was in the places where he found me. And then I would have to listen to his abuse, saying nothing but 'I'm sorry.' To this he would reply, 'You fucking southerners. That's all you ever say! You're sorry.' Once I asked him, ' So what do you northerners say?' He answered, 'How about, "I see what you mean and I won't let it happen again"?' So I started to say, 'I see what you mean and I won't let it happen again' instead of sorry – a lot of times.

The land was dangerous, rugged and wild. There was no such thing as a road, and gullies, rocks and washed-away land surprised you at every given moment. And there was no such thing as a straightforward journey. If I had seen a dinosaur, it wouldn't have looked out of place. And as for the car wheels getting punctures …

Now wherever I laid my hat was my home. For all of that, the routine of any given day wasn't too dissimilar to life on the road with U2, in that the days had no rigid structure and we were always packing up, and hitting the road. The only difference was that U2 went to conquer their fans, and the cowboys went to conquer their cattle.

All mornings began the same, with a 4am cooked breakfast cooked by me. Once I had prepared and cooked the food, I would lay it out on a wooden table that I had placed under a shaded area. The table was collapsible, and was stored along with many other items in the back of the caravan trailer. The morning food was always eaten around the warmth of the campfire. The climate was like that of the desert: hot and sticky during the days; cold to freezing during the nights and early mornings.

When the ringers were in the camp, a billycan of tea was always on the boil. Another of my chores was to fetch fresh water from the creeks, which were an important factor in determining where to set up camp – the priorities being water and shade. Fresh water was needed for cooking, cleaning and bathing oneself. (The ringers always washed themselves in the creeks.)

My short journeys to the creeks were always taken with trepidation, as I scanned the scorched land for snakes and crocodiles. It's amazing how my list of dreaded priorities changed constantly, with snakes no longer being at the top of the list. Dangerous man- eating crocodiles were now my number-one concern.

The only reassuring words that Sterling Buntine gave me were that the crocs swimming about in the water and baking themselves on the side of the banks of the creek were freshwater crocs, and these were not as dangerous as their saltwater relatives – therefore there wasn't a lot to fear. According to Sterling. As far as I was concerned they were still crocodiles and I was going to give them a very wide berth.

It seemed as if everything I did or touched had a sense of imminent danger about it.

Cooking over a naked flame, with no experience of controlling the intensity of the heat, caused me quite a bit of worry. I set fire to many dishes, and once almost to myself. The oven glove that I was wearing had caught fire.

After the morning feed, with the camp emptied of the ringers, I would be left for the entire day to fend for myself, with nothing but the noise of nature ringing about in my head. I had once asked Sterling, in all innocence, what I was to do if I saw a snake, a crocodile or a dingo. Silly me! His answer was … run the other way.

I had always prided myself on having quite a lot of common sense – until I lived out in the bush and experienced back-to-basics survival. Mobiles or any other kind of telephones were non-operational in such remote areas. Occasionally, the satellite phone back on the station picked up a call.

The only noises that ever interrupted the peace of the day would be from the muster-helicopter pilots flying into stock camp for a feed, or the station's supply truck driving into camp to refill my dwindling supplies. Otherwise you never saw another human being.

The long hot, searing days were spent reading recipe books, or writing. And once – when I think I was delirious from the heat – I dared to swim in the creek, allowing myself some respite from the sun.

That was until there was cattle work to be done, and then I would assist the ringers down at the cattle yards, perhaps working the slidings, which were gated holdings that were manually operated. This allowed you to control the flow of cattle once they had been branded and drafted. Other times I would saddle up and ride out to assist the ringers with the muster. I loved it.

But my main priority was cooking and feeding cowboys.

With the temperature burning hot, it was impossible to sit in the sun during the day, so I would take to the shade, under the burnt-up branches of a gum tree. If I wasn't writing, I would be daydreaming, often devising odd jobs in order to keep myself occupied. At times I felt incredibly lonely. The thought that I was insane often drifted into my mind. What other sophisticated city girl in their right mind would dream of undertaking such work?

Once I had acclimatised, I took to wandering away from the camp, thinking myself very brave as I searched about for snappy wood and small gum branches. I would even experiment with different types of menu – a bit of a hit or miss operation. When it missed, it had to be thrown away – as far away from the camp as possible, to avoid invasion by meat-eating ants, dingoes and other wild animals.

Still, I got myself a routine and, with everything almost down to a fine art, had plenty of time to write and daydream.

I was about to discover what Lola Cashman would do next.

I was brought up in a very competitive manner. My dad had always encouraged me in all sports, and at school I had excelled in this area. But I was always taught that to be a good winner, you had to accept defeat graciously. Nevertheless, whatever I chose to do, I always wanted to be the best, and would give anything that I had undertaken my best shot. If I undertook to be a road sweeper, then I would have wanted to be the best road sweeper. If I played a game of chess, it was to win. I was never driven by money alone, and needed to enjoy whatever it was that I was doing, sometimes accepting lowly-paid projects because they sounded fun and rewarding.

I had no great insight into Bono's childhood or upbringing. It was a subject that was never broached, but one thing that was certain was that the man was pugnacious and driven by his fierce passion for justice.

Bono's rewards we are all aware of. And what must be his greatest achievement so far is the fact that he has been nominated for a Nobel peace prize. What more validation could a man want?

To date, it is hard to put on the radio and not hear a U2 song playing. In the same vein he frequently adorns most of the daily press who report on his charitable deeds, and his relentless fights against injustice.

But there is a saying. A man can see a grain of sand on another man's shoulder, but not the hump on his own.

I still haven't found what I'm looking for, but I know I am close.

```
THE EUROPEAN JOSHUA TOUR MAY TO AUGUST 1987
=============================================

     DATE      VENUE/CITY              CAPACITY
     ====      =========               ========
MAY
====
     26TH TUE.
     27TH WED.   ROME, FLAHINO F.STADIUM, ITALY.   50,000.
     28TH THU.
     29TH FRI.   MODENA, BRAGLIA F.STADIUM, ITALY.  35,000.
     30TH SAT.   MODENA, BRAGLIA F.STADIUM, ITALY.  35,000.
     31ST SUN.
JUNE
====
     1ST MON.
     2ND TUE.    LONDON, WEMBLEY ARENA, ENGLAND.   9,000.
     3RD WED.    N.E.C. BIRMINGHAM, ENGLAND.       11,000.
     4TH THU.
     5TH FRI.
     6TH SAT.    GOTHENBURG, ERIKSBERG, SWEDEN.    45,000.
     7TH SUN.
     8TH MON.
     9TH TUE.
     10TH WED.
     12TH FRI.   WEMBLEY STADIUM, LONDON, ENGLAND. 72,000.
     13TH SAT.   WEMBLEY STADIUM, LONDON, ENGLAND. 72,000.
     14TH SUN.
     15TH MON.   PARIS  ZENITH, FRANCE.            6,400.
     16TH TUE.
     17TH WED.   COLOGNE, MUENGERSDORFER.W.GERMANY. 64,285.
     18TH THU.   COLOGNE, MUENGERSDORFER.W.GERMANY. 64,285.
     19TH FRI.
     20TH SAT.
     21ST SUN.   BASEL, FOOTBALL STAD. SWITZERLAND. 45,000.
     22ND MON.
     23RD TUE.
     24TH WED.   BELFAST, THE KINGS HALL, N.IRELAND. 6,000.
     25TH THU.
     26TH FRI.
     27TH SAT.   DUBLIN, CROKE PARK, IRELAND.      60,000.
     28TH SUN.   DUBLIN, CROKE PARK, IRELAND.      60,000.
     29TH MON.
     30TH TUE.
JULY
====
     1ST WED.    LEEDS, ELLAND ROAD, ENGLD.        35,000.
     2ND THU.
     3RD FRI.
     4TH SAT.    PARIS ,DES VINCIENNES, FRANCE.    80,000.
     5TH SUN.    OPTION ON 2ND PARIS SHOW.
     6TH MON.
     7TH TUE.
     8TH WED.    BRUSSELS,FOREST NATIONALE, BELGIUM.12,000.
     9TH THU.
     10TH FRI.   FEYENOORD STAD, ROTTERDAM.HOLLAND. 50,000.
     11TH SAT.   FEYENOORD STAD, ROTTERDAM.HOLLAND. 50,000.
     12TH SUN.
```

```
     13TH MON.
     14TH TUE.
     15TH WED.   REAL MADRID STADIUM, SPAIN.       50,000.
     16TH THU.
     17TH FRI.
     18TH SAT.   MONTPELIER, ESP.RICHTER, FRANCE.  35,000.
     19TH SUN.
     20TH MON.
     21TH TUE.   MUNICH, OLYMPICHALLE.  W.GERMANY. 10,000.
     22ND WED.   MUNICH, OLYMPICHALLE.  W.GERMANY. 10,000.
     23RD THU.
     24TH FRI.
     25TH SAT.   CARDIFF ARMS PARK, WALES.         55,000.
     26TH SUN.
     27TH MON.
     28TH TUE.
     29TH WED.   GLASGOW, S.E.C. SCOTLAND.         10,000.
     30TH THU.   GLASGOW, S.E.C. SCOTLAND.         10,000.
     31ST FRI.
AUGUST.
======
     1ST SAT.    EDINBURGH, MURRATFIELD, SCOTLAND. 45,000.
     2ND SUN.
     3RD MON.    BIRMINGHAM, N.E.C. ENGLAND.       11,000.
     4TH TUE.    BIRMINGHAM, N.E.C. ENGLAND.       11,000.
     5TH WED.
     6TH THU.
     7TH FRI.
     8TH SAT.    CORK, PAIRC A UI CHAOIMH, IRELAND. 45,000.
     9TH SUN.

     ZZZZZZZZZZZZZZZZZZZZZZZZZZZZZZZZZZZZZZZZZZZZZZZZZZZZZZZ
```

```
                    U2 TOUR PERSONNEL
                    ================

        NAME                                NAT/TY   TAG NO.
1.   Adam Clayton                           UK       7
2.   David Evans                            UK       2
3.   Paul Hewson                            IRL      1
4.   Larry Mullen Jnr.                      IRL      4

5.   Paul McGuiness       Manager           UK       3

6.   Dennis Sheehan       Tour Manager      UK       5
7.   Bob Koch             Tour Accountant   US       8
8.   Ellen Darst          Management Associat US     6
9.   Keryn Kaplan         Assistant/Ellen Darst IRL  9
10.  Suzanne Doyle        Guest Co-Ordinator  US
11.  Bob Wein             Chief of Security   US
12.  Jim Singleton        Advance & Concert Sec. UK  12
13.  John Clark           Group Security      US      15
14.  Mike Andy            Group Security      UK
15.  Lola Cashman         Wardrobe            IRL     28
16.  Fintan Fitzgerald    Wardrobe/Hairdresser USA
17.  Theresa Pesce        Travel Co-ordinator

CREW
====
        NAME                                NAT.    TAG NO.
1    Steve Iredale        Production Manager  IRL     16
2    Joe O'Herlihy        House Sound Engineer IRL    17
3    Peter Williams       Lighting Designer   UK      20
4    Tim Buckley          Stage Manager       IRL     18
5    Tom Mullally         Production Assistant UK     21
6    Dez Broadbery        Keyboard Technician  IRL    22
7    Sam O'Sullivan       Drum Technician      UK      23
8    Guitar Roadie        Guitar Technician    US      25
9    Bob Loney            Tour Technician      IRL     24
10   Adam Rankin          Bono and Stage       IRL     53
11   Frazer McAlister     Guitar Technician    UK
12   Torq Buckley         Carpenter

13   Jo Ravitch           Clair Bros.P.A.      US      29
14   Dave Wilkerson       Clair Bros.P.A.      US      30
15   C.J.Patterson        Clair Bros.P.A.      US      31
16   Dave Skaff           Clair Bros.P.A.      US      32
17   Billy Louthe         Clair Bros.P.A.      IRL     33
18   Jeff Stein           Clair Bros.P.A.      US
19   Christopher Fulton   Clair Bros.P.A.      US
20   James Bang           Clair Bros.P.A.      US

21   Scott Richmond       Nocturne lights(o/d)  US     35
22   Dave Baker           Nocturne lights(o/d)  US     37

23   Phelim McMahon       Supermick Lights(all) UK
24   Julian Watkins       Supermick Lights(all) UK
25   Chris Lambourne      Supermick Lights(o/d) UK
26   Lynne Scottin        Supermick Lights(o/d) UK
27   Andrew Stacey        Supermick Lights(o/d) UK
28   Fearse Ellis         Supermick Lights(o/d) UK
```

```
29   Peter Jennings       Supermick Lights(i/d)  UK
30   Richard Gallup       Supermick Lights(i/d)  UK
31   Ian Tuell            Supermick Lights(i/d)  UK
32   Jim Lawford          Supermick Lights(i/d)  UK

33   Steve Witwer         Rigger 1               USA    40
34   Bill Spoon           Rigger 11              USA    41

35   Paul Vissor          Catering               UK
36   Muffat Vissor        Catering               UK
37   Susan Aris           Catering               UK

38   John Kennedy         Stage Prod.Mgr.        IRL
39   Peter Clarke         Advance Production     UK

40   Paul Henries         Eurotrux(o/d)          UK
41   Nick Mallett         Eurotrux(o/d)          UK
42   Stephen Clarke       Eurotrux(o/d)          UK
43   Philip Pearce        Eurotrux(o/d)          UK
44   Kenneth Rich         Eurotrux(o/d)          UK
45   Kevin Barnes         Eurotrux(o/d)          UK
46   Julian Nash          Eurotrux(o/d)          UK
47   Steve Manning        Eurotrux(o/d)          UK
48   Shift Driver 1       Eurotrux(i/d)          UK
49   Shift Driver 2       Eurotrux(i/d)          UK
50   Shift driver 3       Eurotrux(i/d)          UK

51   Colin Barratt        London Pullman
52   Keith Roper          London Pullman         UK
53   Dave Parsons         London Pullman         UK
54   Mgnt Bus             London Pullman         UK

55   Mr.Bell and Eades    HS 125 Captains
56   Fletcher             First Officer          UK
57   Melanie White        Stewardess             UK

58 AND UP ****************

    European Grid Systems and Upfront Staging crew members.
    Eurotrux arctics with EGS/Upfront.
    Not Us Merchandising (Chris Parkos, John Panaro )

                  THATS ALL FOLKS!!!!!!!!!!!

ZZZZZZZZZZZZZZZZZZZZZZZZZZZZZZZZZZZZZZZZZZZZZZZZZZZZZZZZZZZZ
```

U.S.A. TOUR, APRIL-MAY 1987

APRIL

1	A.S.U. EVENTS CENTRE PRODUCTION REHEARSAL.
2	A.S.U. EVENTS CENTRE, TEMPE, ARIZONA.
3	A.S.U. EVENTS CENTRE, TEMPE, ARIZONA.
4	THE COMMUNITY CENTRE, TUCSON, ARIZONA.
5	DAY OFF. TRAVEL DAY.
6	DAY OFF. TRAVEL DAY.
7	THE SUMMIT, HOUSTON, TEXAS.
8	THE SUMMIT, HOUSTON, TEXAS.
9	DAY OFF. TRAVEL DAY.
10	PAN AM CENTRE, LAS CRUCES, NEW MEXICO.
11	DAY OFF. TRAVEL DAY.
12	THOMAS AND MACK ARENA, LAS VEGAS, NEVADA.
13	S.D. SPORTS ARENA, SAN DIEGO, CALIFORNIA.
14	S.D. SPORTS ARENA, SAN DIEGO, CALIFORNIA.
15	DAY OFF. TRAVEL DAY.
16	DAY OFF.
17	L.A. SPORTS ARENA, LOS ANGELES, CALIFORNIA.
18	L.A. SPORTS ARENA, LOS ANGELES, CALIFORNIA.
19	DAY OFF
20	L.A. SPORTS ARENA, LOS ANGELES, CALIFORNIA.
21	L.A. SPORTS ARENA, LOS ANGELES, CALIFORNIA.
22	L.A. SPORTS ARENA, LOS ANGELES, CALIFORNIA.
23	DAY OFF. TRAVEL DAY.
24	THE COW PALACE, SAN FRANCISCO, CALIFORNIA.
25	THE COW PALACE, SAN FRANCISCO, CALIFORNIA.
26	DAY OFF. TRAVEL DAY.
27	DAY OFF.
28	DAY OFF.
29	THE ROSEMONT HORIZON, CHICAGO, ILLINOIS.
30	THE SILVERDOME, PONTIAC, MICHIGAN.

MAY

1	DAY OFF. TRAVEL DAY.
2	THE CENTRUM, WORCESTER, MASSACHUSETTS.
3	THE CENTRUM, WORCESTER, MASSACHUSETTS.
4	THE CENTRUM, WORCESTER, MASSACHUSETTS.
5	DAY OFF. TRAVEL DAY

(CONTINUED) U.S.A. TOUR, APRIL-MAY 1987

MAY

6	THE CIVIC CENTRE, HARTFORD, CONNECTICUT.(HOLD).
7	THE CIVIC CENTRE, HARTFORD, CONNECTICUT.
8	THE CIVIC CENTRE, HARTFORD, CONNECTICUT.
9	THE CIVIC CENTRE, HARTFORD, CONNECTICUT.
10	DAY OFF. TRAVEL DAY.
11	BRENDAN BYRNE ARENA, EAST RUTHERFORD, NEW JERSEY.
12	BRENDAN BYRNE ARENA, EAST RUTHERFORD, NEW JERSEY.
13	BRENDAN BYRNE ARENA, EAST RUTHERFORD, NEW JERSEY.
14	DAY OFF.
15	BRENDAN BYRNE ARENA, EAST RUTHERFORD, NEW JERSEY.
16	BRENDAN BYRNE ARENA, EAST RUTHERFORD, NEW JERSEY.
17	FINISH TOUR. RETURN TO HOME BASE.
	17th-25th of MAY OFF.
27	START OF EURO-TOUR, ROME

(CONTINUED) U.S.A. TOUR, APRIL-MAY 1987

MAY

6	THE CIVIC CENTRE, HARTFORD, CONNECTICUT.(HOLD).
7	THE CIVIC CENTRE, HARTFORD, CONNECTICUT.
8	THE CIVIC CENTRE, HARTFORD, CONNECTICUT.
9	THE CIVIC CENTRE, HARTFORD, CONNECTICUT.
10	DAY OFF. TRAVEL DAY.
11	BRENDAN BYRNE ARENA, EAST RUTHERFORD, NEW JERSEY.
12	BRENDAN BYRNE ARENA, EAST RUTHERFORD, NEW JERSEY.
13	BRENDAN BYRNE ARENA, EAST RUTHERFORD, NEW JERSEY.
14	DAY OFF.
15	BRENDAN BYRNE ARENA, EAST RUTHERFORD, NEW JERSEY.
16	BRENDAN BYRNE ARENA, EAST RUTHERFORD, NEW JERSEY.
17	FINISH TOUR. RETURN TO HOME BASE.
	17th-25th of MAY OFF.
27	START OF EURO-TOUR, ROME

GROUP AND MANAGEMENT

		BAGGAGE TAG NUMBER
PAUL HEWSON	VOCALS, GUITAR, HARMONICA	
DAVID EVANS	GUITAR, KEYBOARDS, VOCALS	1
ADAM CLAYTON	BASS GUITAR, BASS SYNTH PEDALS	2
LARRY MULLEN	DRUMS, VOCALS	7
		4
PAUL McGUINNESS	MANAGER	
ELLEN DARST	MANAGEMENT ASSOCIATE	3
DENNIS SHEEHAN	TOUR MANAGER	6
BOB KOCH	TOUR ACCOUNTANT	5
KERVN KAPLIN	PRINCIPLE MGNT. U.S.A.	8
PAUL WASSERMAN	PRESS CO-ORDINATOR	9
ALVENIA BRIDGES	TOUR PRESS	42
MARC COLEMAN	PERSONAL ASSISTANT TO GROUP	11
		10
JIM SINGLETON	SECURITY CO-ORDINATOR	
JOHN CLARK	GROUP SECURITY	12
MIKE ANDY	GROUP SECURITY	14
		15
CHRIS PARKES	U2 MERCHANDISING.	
		44

COACHES

JACK LAPP	LEAD DRIVER (FLORIDA CUSTOM COACH WEST)
BERNIE THORNE	DRIVER
RED JILLIAN	DRIVER

PLANE

ROBIN PITTOCK	PILOT
	NAVIGATOR
JEAN PITTOCK	STEWARDESS

WINTERLAND MERCHANDISING CREW

STEVE HITTSON
COLLEEN HITTSON